The Highways and Byways of Life

Volume 3

One hundred road signs to refresh and reinvigorate us

Philip M. Hudson

Copyright 2020 by Philip M. Hudson.

Published 2020.

Printed in the United States of America.

All rights reserved.

No portion of this book may be reproduced, stored in a retrieval system, or transmitted in any form or by any means – electronic, mechanical, photocopy, recording, scanning, or other – except for brief quotations in critical reviews or articles, without the prior written permission of the author.

ISBN 978-1-950647-67-5

Illustrations – Google Images.

This book may be ordered from online bookstores.

Publishing Services by BookCrafters
Parker, Colorado.
www.bookcrafters.net

Table of Contents

Foreword..1
Introduction..3

Right Turn Only...7
Road Closed...11
Road Closed to Thru Traffic...15
Road Ends..19
Road Narrows...23
Rough Road Ahead..27
Roundabout Ahead..31
Rumble Strips Ahead...33
Scenic Area..39
Scenic Byway..43
School Bus Stop Ahead..49
School Zone..53
Secure Your Load...57
See Tracks / Think Train...61
Severe Weather..67
Share The Road..71
Sharp Curves..75
Sidewalk Closed...79
Signal Ahead..83
Signal Operation Changed..87
Slight Curve Ahead...91
Slippery When Wet...97
Slow...99

Slow: Blind Curve Ahead	103
Slow: Construction Ahead	107
Slow Down	111
Slow Down at Night	115
Slow Down: Obey Speed Limit	119
Slow Down: Uncontrolled Intersection Ahead	121
Slow Down: Only You Can Prevent Speed Bumps	127
Slower Traffic Keep Right	131
Slow: Road Under Repair	133
Slow: Rough Road Ahead	135
Slow Vehicles Use Right Lane	141
Smiles to Go Before We Sleep	145
Speed Cameras	149
Speed Checked By Radar	151
Speed Limit	155
Speed Reduced Ahead	159
Speed Up	165
Stay Awake	171
Stay in Your Lane	175
Steep Grade Ahead	179
Stop Ahead	183
Stop Complaining	187
Stop Distracted Driving	191
Stop Drowsy Driving	197
Stop Gossiping	199
Stop Grumbling	201
Stop, Look, and Listen	205
Take Responsibility	209
Thank You For Slowing Down	215
The Future: Just Ahead	219
Think Before You Speak	221

Thru Traffic: Merge Right 225
Tough Decisions Ahead 229
Tow Away Zone 235
Traction Tires Required 239
Traffic Fines Double in Work Zones 241
Traffic Islands Ahead 245
Train Depot 251
Trucks & Heavy Vehicles: Balance Your Load 255
Trucks: Right Lane Only 261
Try Your Brakes 265
Turn On Headlights For Safety 269
Two Way Traffic 271
Under Construction 275
Uneven Lanes 279
Uneven Road Surface 281
Unplanned Detour 285
Viewpoint Ahead 289
Vision Just Ahead 293
Visitor Information 295
Warning: Avalanche Area 299
Warning: I Do Dumb Things 303
Warning: I May Look Calm 307
Warp Drive 311
Watch Downhill Speed 317
Watch For Congestion Ahead 321
Watch For Emergency Vehicles 323
Watch For Farm Machinery 327
Watch For Oncoming Traffic 331
Watch For Pedestrians 333
Watch For School Bus 337
Watch For Wildlife 341

Wedding Season Ahead	345
Weigh Station	347
Weight Restriction Notice	349
Welcome	353
Welcome To A New Beginning	355
We Reserve The Right To Refuse Service To Anyone	361
Wheelchair Access	365
Where am I?	369
Where Is Everybody?	373
Wildlife Crossing	377
Wind Gusts	381
Winding Road	387
Work In Progress	389
Wrong Way	391
Wrong Way – Go Back	395
Yield	399
Yield To Oncoming Traffic	403
Yield To Pedestrians Ahead	405
Afterword	409
Appendix One	415
Appendix Two	449
About The Author	457
By The Author	459
What More Can I Say?	463

Foreword

When negotiating the Highways
and Byways of Life, we are likely
to encounter a variety of road signs
that help to smoothly regulate the course
of our journeys, as well as to warn us of
impending danger during our travels. We
are familiar with these signs, although
we may not have previously though
of them in the way described in
this book. After reading about
their hidden meanings, you
may forever look at
them differently.

Introduction

"Brevity is the soul of wit." (Shakespeare, "Hamlet," Act 2, Scene 4). It is the economical use of words in speech or writing. As I consider the one hundred selections in this anthology, I fear that I have been verbose.

Paul encouraged his friend Timothy to "shun profane and vain babblings" in his communication. (2 Timothy 2:16). Such thoughtless exercises are nothing more than prattle and are detrimental to our intellectual and spiritual health. A good rule of thumb is that "any philosophy that can be put in a nutshell belongs there." (Branch Rickey). An example is this twelve-word encapsulation of the Gospel: "I came into the world to do the will of my Father." (3 Nephi 27:13). God's mission statement is comparably brief: "This is my work and my glory, to bring to pass the immortality and eternal life of man." (Moses 1:39).

We should strive to craft our message without giving "heed to fables and endless genealogies, which minister questions." (1 Timothy 1:4). Our written communications should be focused and purposeful. "The most valuable of all talents," declared Thomas Jefferson, "is that of never using two words when one will do." We've all heard someone say: "I would have to answer that in the affirmative", and have thought to ourselves that a simple "Yes" would have done quite well, thank you! When we accept such chicanery as normal, our hearts wax gross, our ears become dull of hearing, and we close our eyes. (See Matthew 13:15).

"Brevity is the best recommendation of speech, whether in a senator or an orator." (Cicero). "If any man teach otherwise, and consent not to wholesome words ... he is proud, knowing nothing, but doting about questions and strifes of words, whereof cometh envy, ... railings, evil surmisings, perverse disputings of men of corrupt minds, and destitute of the truth, supposing that gain is godliness." (1 Timothy 6:3-5).

Carelessness in our speech opens the floodgates of banality, leading to a rising tide of unremarkable words that are tedious, trivial, and predictable, that lack originality, interest and excitement.

"Brevity is a great charm of eloquence." (Cicero). "The words of wise men are heard in quiet more than the cry of him that ruleth among fools." (Ecclesiastes 9:17). When perspiration precedes inspiration, the spirit leads us to the four basic characteristics of interpersonal communication: clarity, simplicity, brevity, and humanity. "There is need of brevity, that the thought may run on." (Horace). Less is more. Seeds are small in comparison to the harvest.

Brevity can throw open the floodgates of the mind. It can be the key that unlocks the door leading to the brightly lighted avenues of inquiry. "Spartans, stoics, heroes, saints and gods use short and positive speech," declared Ralph

Waldo Emerson. All the great things are simple, and many can be expressed in a single word: charity, code, duty, freedom, honor, hope, love, justice, mercy, sacrifice, and service.

We intuitively know when words have had their desired impact. "Thus saith the still small voice, which whispereth through and pierceth all things," without belaboring the point, "and often times it maketh (our) bones to quake while it maketh manifest" without overanalyzing or exhausting the subject. (D&C 85:6).

This introduction, by the way, has 599 words, but the longest reflection in this volume, ironically, is "Take Responsibility". It is a real heavyweight, at 1,120 words. Forgive me, dear reader, for being so loquacious; for not having taken Shakespeare's advice in such wordy instances. In some cases, though, I succeeded. The shortest musing, interestingly enough, is "Stop Gossiping", weighing in at just 127 words.

Right Turn Only

Because
there must needs be
opposition in all things,
our obedience to the road
signs along the Highways and
Byways of Life encouraging us
to make Right Turns Only is all
the more important. Because we
are also free to turn left, and
follow the road that leads to
Apostasy, we need to remain
steadfast as we determine
to choose the right
way to go.

The Savior uses the laws of the physical universe to help us to make good choices. Natural digression in the temporal world from order to disorder suits His purpose as long as it jars us out of our collective complacency. (See Matthew 10:34-38). This unrest upsets the status quo, gets us thinking, prods us to expend our energy purposefully, and constructively put our agency to work.

Progress becomes the recompense for perseverance, salvation is the reward for surmounting obstacles, and the hope of eternal life is the blessing for enduring opposition. By experience, we learn that Gospel principles that relate to the eternities can supersede physical laws that relate only to the temporal universe. By choosing the right, we become new creatures in Christ, oriented more to the laws of the eternal world and the commandments of the Master than to the limitations imposed by the physical world. Our experience is inexplicable, and yet undeniable. "Whatsoever is born of God overcometh the (law of opposition governing the physical) world." (1 John 5:3).

Nevertheless, for as long as we journey along the Highways and Byways of Life, even as we determine to make Right Turns Only, other laws governing the physical universe that may not seem to be oriented in that direction must still be honored. Our submission to seemingly destructive laws creates the opportunity to be obedient to clearly constructive laws with a potential to assist us to reach even greater heights that could not otherwise have been attained. It seems that without opposition at work, God would cease to be God, in the sense that He could not bring to pass our immortality and eternal life. (See 2 Nephi 2:11-13 & Moses 1:39).

Opposition is the companion of spiritual growth. By confronting it, we gain the confidence to sacrifice temporal things in order to overcome the physical world, and to allow the law of eternal progression to trump negative or destructive forces in our lives.

On our journey along the Highways and Byways of Life, we learn to appreciate how hard it is to forsake the supposed security and comfort of the world. The signs that lure us to deviate to the left exert a power over us that is sometimes hard to control. Therefore, the Lord has revealed a basic truth, that makes it easier to choose to only turn to the right. Specifically, when we obtain any blessing from God, it is by obedience to the law upon which it is predicated." (D&C 130:21). "For all who will have a blessing at my hands", He said, "shall abide the law which was appointed for that blessing, and the conditions thereof, as were instituted from before the foundation of the world." (D&C 132:5). We learn to relate obedience to blessings, and we discover that commandments and blessings are synonymous.

Paul urged the Galatian Saints not to be deceived. "God is not mocked: for whatsoever a man soweth, that shall he also reap. For he that soweth to his flesh shall of the flesh reap corruption; but he that soweth to the Spirit shall of the Spirit reap life everlasting." (Galatians 6:7-8). With blood, sweat, and tears we toil to obtain temporal treasures, sacrificing even those things that are near and dear to us, but at the last day entropy still demands physical destruction, while its opposite, that is defined by choosing the right, promises the blessing of eternal progression.

Since most of us have not yet made the leap of faith to become the architects of our own fate, we are commanded to give our language "to exhortation continually", that we might not become "weary in well doing." (D&C 23:7 & Galatians 6:9). Because the principle of opposition is so powerful in the physical universe, those of us who have been born again still require constant and repetitive encouragement in our quest to unflinchingly Turn to The Right.

Road Closed

As we travel the
Highways and Byways of
Life, we may occasionally
encounter Road Closed signs,
but we need not fear that
because we do so, our
way will be hedged
or our progress
impeded.

The power of the ordinances of the Gospel and of our related covenants is so great that it will show us the way along the Highways and Byways of Life, even if it seems unclear. That power enables us to disorient our adversaries, giving us time to evade their evil designs and machinations, successfully complete our mortal missions, and return with honor to our heavenly home.

As Joseph Smith received instruction relating to how he should proceed, the meaning and intent of the scriptures was opened to his understanding, so much so that he could actually comprehend the mind and will of God. (See D&C 76:12). For him, there were no road closures. On the contrary, the word of the Lord opened up avenues of understanding that he could, heretofore, have scarcely appreciated. With truth, light, and Spirit, "even the Spirit of Jesus Christ", he may have been the first mortal to explode the myth that we use only 10% of our brain power. (D&C 84:45). He came to regularly enjoy a many fold increase of the illumination in his mind of principles that had previously been difficult for him to understand.

As we mature in the Gospel, the unknown possibilities of existence will crystallize in our brains, as well. We will be transformed so that we might better understand that "intelligence cleaveth unto intelligence; wisdom receiveth wisdom; truth embraceth truth; virtue loveth virtue; light cleaveth unto light; mercy ... claimeth her own; justice continueth its course, (and) judgment goeth before the face of him who sitteth upon the throne." (D&C 88:40).

When we encounter road closures during our journey, the Spirit will increase the light with breathtaking clarity. In visions splendid, we will be on our way attended by the Holy Ghost, but only if we keep ourselves worthy and choose wisely, avoiding dead-ends, distracting detours, and closed roads on the Highways and Byways of Life. If we keep the commandments, we will receive "light, until (we are) glorified in truth and knoweth all things." (D&C 93:28).

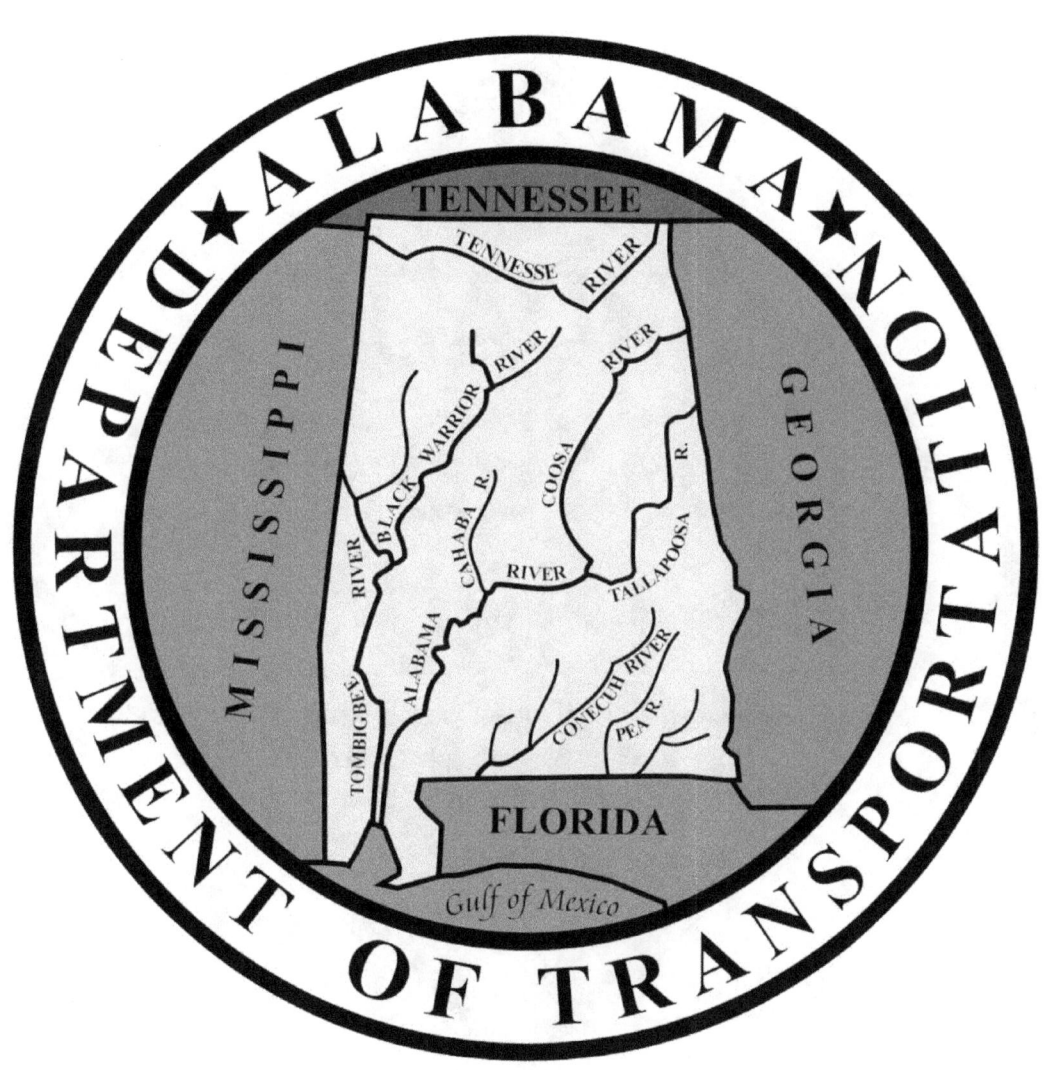

Road Closed To Thru Traffic

The only roads that have been permanently closed to thru traffic on the Highways and Byways of Life are those that would lead us to the confusion of religious roundabouts, conceptual cul-de-sacs, and doctrinal dead ends.

In a world that is filled with smoke and mirrors and artful deception, we will be able to clearly see what is real only if we remain on the strait and narrow way that affords us a more spiritually advantageous point of view

Roads that are Closed to Thru Traffic generally follow a sketchy path on the slippery slope just above personality precipices. They lead to nowhere, and along the way travelers are tossed to and fro and carried about with every wind of doctrine by the sleight of men and cunning craftiness. The monotony of the landscape adjacent to Roads that are Closed to Thru Traffic be hypnotic, leading to a stupor of thought.

If we choose to go down that path, sooner or later, we will become incapable of independent action. We will begin to look forward to the gentle caress of the flaxen cords around our necks that are leading us to our fate. We will have lost the desire, and perhaps the capacity, to turn around and retrace our steps to the safety of the highway. Only too late, we will find that we have allowed these silken materials that initially had felt so comfortable to be transformed into iron chains that drag us down to hell.

Road Ends

Some people
think that it's the
end of the road when they
have to perform any labor that
is outside their comfort zone. They
are not accustomed to sacrifice,
nor have they experienced the
blessings associated with
unrequited giving.

As we move along on the Highways and Byways of Life, our discipleship will demand that we pause along the way to build altars that will become bridges between heaven and earth. It is there that we will determine to make sacrifice to the gods. We do so, knowing that what has been profaned may become sacred.

We look forward to the day when the road will end and we will receive a gift that no one can take from us. We will be as "brave Horatius, the Captain of the Gate", who declared: "To each of us upon this earth, death cometh soon or late. And how can we die better than facing fearful odds, for the ashes of our fathers, and the temples of our gods?" ("Lays of Ancient Rome", Thomas Babbington Macaulay).

Although one road may end, another avenue will open up before us, as our nature is made sacred, or holy. Our sacrifice of a broken heart and a contrite spirit will have accustomed us to partaking of the emblems of Christ, which will make sacred our petitions to the Lord and be as a talisman of truth.

The Greek word for "healing" originally meant, "sacrifice to the gods." Our sacrifices will become expressions of our commitment to consecration, to sacrifice to our God, Who will heal our broken spirits. If He continues to smile upon us, and the road ahead does not end, just yet, our continuing dedication to sacrifice will ennoble us to walk in the light of the Lord ever closer to our destiny.

Road Narrows

If mortality could be visualized in spatial dimensions, it would take the shape of an hourglass, with the strait gate its narrow midsection.

After passing through that constriction, unparalleled vistas would open up to reveal untapped potential and unparalleled opportunity. But initially, many of us would be caught in conceptually confusing cul-de-sacs that would prevent us from comprehending the purpose of The Plan. We would wander to and fro, dazed and disoriented, like flotsam and jetsam on the sea of life.

Some of us would be stalled in telestial traffic jams that would overheat our engines, foul our lubricants, seize our moving parts, and restrict our access to freely flowing spiritual energy. Others would lack restraint, as if their brake pads were worn, interfering with their ability to slow down in order to avoid the sand traps of transgression as they negotiated the minefields of mortality. Their ability to move forward with purpose might be compromised. With their gears grinding and their clutch plates slipping, they might lose their traction as they tried to move upward.

A few of us might squander scarce resources, as if our

thermostats were inoperable, allowing our cooling systems to boil over from the excitement of excessive exertion in the steam plant of sin. All these mechanical issues might combine to overwhelm us in a perfect storm of trial and temptation, forcing, as it were, lifestyle compromises that would make self-control all the more difficult, while making rationalization a more tempting option.

But for the few of us who would be lucky enough to finally reach the constriction in the hourglass on the Highways and Byways of Life, there would come a realization that the time to stand and deliver had arrived. As Brutus observed, we would face that "tide in the affairs of men which, taken at the flood, leads on to fortune. Omitted", we would realize that the voyage of our lives would be condemned to be "bound in shallows and in miseries. On such a full sea", however, we would find ourselves "afloat, and we" would "take the current when it serves, or lose our ventures." (Shakespeare, "Julius Caesar", Act 4, Scene 3).

Those who made it through the strait and narrow way would be fortunate, indeed, to find that by following the blueprints of The Plan, they would be given enough wiggle-room to be able to successfully flex their spiritual muscles and exercise their moral agency in a forum of free will that engaged opposition in a vigorous tug-of-war. They would realize that travel upon the Highways and Byways of Life plays out best when its participants are able to make good choices in the midst of less attractive competing options. They would hope to be sensitive to spiritual promptings, to be stimulated by the light of Christ, to receive the Gift of the Holy Ghost, to be thereby guided, and to be replenished with the high octane fuel of faith that would ignite the fire of their fortitude and propel them forward on their journey.

Those who would seize the moment, thread the eye of the needle, and negotiate the strait and narrow path would realize that what at the outset had felt like a confinement and a constraint, as the Road Narrowed, was in fact a birth canal, or a portal through which all must pass in order to progress eternally. They would feel as if they had literally been born again. Expanding circles of opportunity that had beforehand been hidden from their view would snap into sharp focus. They would see beyond the limited horizon of their sight to comprehend a vision in which the perfect law of liberty stretched out before them in a vista of incomprehensible proportion. They would see that the Highways and Byways of Life rest on solid footings that are reinforced with the rebar of resolve, and that it is upon the foundation of faith, and of the covenants that we make with Him, that celestial sureties are constructed, leading to eternal life in His mansions above.

Rough Road

The highways and byways of life are defined by the road to repentance.

The miracle is that when we choose to follow that road, from among many on the Highways and Byways of Life, we engage in a partnership with God. With His Spirit to guide us, we draw upon powers and reserves that are greater than ourselves, to become the architects of our own fate. Perhaps Victor Hugo heard that majestic clockwork when he wrote: "Be like a bird that pausing in her flight a while on boughs to light, feels them give way beneath her, and yet sings, knowing that she hath wings." Repentance facilitates our engagement, in the armory of thought, with fashioning weapons to defend our faith. With these tools, the Lord will show us how to fortify heavenly mansions of joy and strength and peace.

Repentance allows us to become "the shapers of condition, environment, and destiny." (Spencer W. Kimball, "The Miracle of Forgiveness", p. 103). As we repent, even though the road before us might be uphill most of the way, angels will attend us. "For I will go before your face", promised the Lord. "I will be on your right hand, and on your left, and my Spirit shall be in your hearts, and mine angels round about you, to bear you up." (D&C 84:88). When we experience the holy anointing of forgiveness, we will "never rest until the last enemy is conquered, (spiritual) death has been destroyed, and truth reigns triumphant." (Parley P. Pratt, "Deseret News", 4/30/1853).

Roundabout Ahead

There is
no uncertainty or
confusion in the minds
of the faithful regarding
where they are going or the
route they should be following
because they are the children
of a God Who knows each
of them personally, and
Who takes an interest
in each of them, thru
the Holy Ghost.

They know what it means to be about their Father's business. They are not caught in an endless loop, on the Highways and Byways of Life. When Alice was in Wonderland, she asked the Cheshire Cat: "Would you please tell me which way I ought to go from here?" The Cat responded: "That depends a good deal on where you want to go." Alice acknowledged: "I admit, I don't much care where." To which the cat retorted: "Then it doesn't matter which way you go." Alice implored: "Just so I go somewhere!" The cat observed: "Oh, you are sure to do that, if you only walk far enough."

Rumble Strips Ahead

It has been
said that "some
wish to live within sight
of a chapel; others wish to
serve a mission within a yard
of hell." It may not make
any difference, because
the easy times may
be behind us.

In the Twenty-first Century, it is sobering to reflect upon the sacrifices of those whose blood has been shed in the defense of religious expression and free speech. To safeguard these inalienable rights today, we often take our cases to impartial courts, but it was not always so. Every time we open our mouths to state our opinion, every time we read a controversial book, every time we post our thoughts of social media, every time we do a Google search on an interesting topic, we have men like William Tyndale to thank, who gave his life to first establish, and then to protect, and finally to preserve our expressions and our desire for unhindered religious scholarship, all in the comfort of our native tongue.

Listen to William Tyndale: "It is God's gift, to suffer for Christ's sake. Happy are ye if ye suffer for the name of

Christ; for the glorious Spirit of God resteth in you. Is it not an happy thing, to be sure that thou art sealed with God's Spirit to everlasting life? And, verily, thou art sure thereof, if thou suffer patiently for his sake. Tribulation maketh feeling; or it maketh us feel the goodness of God, and his help, and the working of his Spirit. Lo, Christ is never strong in us till we be weak. As our strength abateth, so groweth the strength of Christ in us. Therefore, very gladly will I rejoice in my weakness, that the strength of Christ may dwell in me."

On another occasion, Tyndale wrote: "Behold, God setteth before us a blessing and also a curse: a blessing, if we suffer tribulation and adversity with our Lord and Savior Christ; and an everlasting curse, if, for a little pleasure's sake, we withdraw ourselves from the chastising and nurture of God, wherewith he teacheth all his sons, and fashioneth them after his godly will, and maketh them perfect, and maketh them apt and meet vessels to receive his grace and his Spirit."

When we study his translations and writings, we sense the portent of his own martyrdom, but more significantly, we are enveloped in the fire of his words that brim over with an enthusiastic expectation of unspeakable joy. He was as Jeremiah, who wrote: "But his word was in mine heart as a burning fire shut up in my bones, and I was weary with forbearing, and I could not stop." (K.J.V. Jeremiah 20:9). Or, as Tyndale wrote in his Old Testament translation: "But the word of the Lord was a very burning fire in my heart and

in my bones, which when I would have stopped, I might not."
(Tyndale Bible, Jeremiah 20:9).

He made little or no distinction between the anticipation of eternal happiness in the resurrection and the realization of joy, or more properly, hope, during his sojourn through this vale of tears. His faith was firmly based on that hope, which gave him the ability to see things as they really are. Consequently, he enjoyed a confidence that was not dependent upon circumstances. "It is a plain earnest that there is no other way into the kingdom of life than through persecution, and suffering of pain, and of very death, after the ensample of Christ; therefore, let us arm our souls with the comfort of the scriptures: how that God is ever ready a hand, in time of need, to help us; and how that such tyrants and persecutors are but God's scourge, and His rod to chastise us." Faced with that sense of determination, his tormenters could never gain the upper hand, for in his mind they were special friends sent from God to try him and to prove him, and to make sure that he was worthy of his hire.

He may have been something of a fatalist, but it cannot be disputed that he was somehow completely at ease with the memory of his former life and the purpose of his call, and that he never wavered in his zealous determination to fulfill a mission whose objective was clearly defined in his own mind. He persevered because he was sure of his election as a servant of the Lord Jesus Christ, and it seems that, particularly in his darkest hours, his Master had already invited him to come and "sup with Him." (Tyndale Bible, Revelation 3:20). The Savior had granted His faithful servant a peace that surpasses our understanding. "Let us receive all things of God", he encouraged, "whether it be good or bad: let us humble ourselves under his mighty hand, and submit ourselves unto his nurture and chastising, and not withdraw ourselves from his correction."

The conduct of Tyndale's life expressed a peace born of confident expectation. "He will not work until all be past remedy", he wrote, "and brought unto such a case, that men may see, how that his hand, his power, his mercy, his goodness and truth, hath wrought altogether. He will let no man be partaker with him of his praise and glory. His works are wonderful, and contrary unto man's works. Who ever, saving he, delivered his own Son, his only Son, his dear Son, unto the death, and that for his enemies' sake, to win his enemy, to overcome him with love, that he might see love, and love again, and of love do likewise to other men, and overcome them with well doing?"

There may be Rumble Strips Ahead, on the Highways and Byways of life. God grant that we do not have to fight the same battles that William Tyndale fought, but more importantly, God grant us the faith to meet our challenges head-on, as he did, and to deal with them as graciously as he did.

Scenic Area

The Highways
and Byways of Life
follow a divine design
that takes us on a journey
through areas of breathtaking
scenery. We have been given the
Light of Christ and the Holy Ghost
to add vibrancy to a colorful palate
that has been custom created by our
Heavenly Father with us in mind
and for our enjoyment.

Heavenly Father knew that darkness would ooze out from destructive dominions that would threaten to disrupt our spiritual symmetry, creating a cascade effect of negative energy and culminating in a stupor of thought. As Samuel the Lamanite asked: "How long will ye suffer yourselves to be led by foolish and blind guides? Yea, how long will ye choose darkness rather than light?" (Helaman 13:29). If we were to try to reach our destination by relying upon only the illumination provided by the dim light of the moon, it would be nigh unto impossible. If we were fortunate, we might just be able to make out the glimmering facets of the light of the Spirit, but we would still be likely to stumble over hidden obstacles, and fall from grace.

The glow of the Light of Christ may be likened to the

microwave background radiation from the Big Bang that permeates the universe. At 2.76° Kelvin, it is better than nothing at all, but arguably, since it hovers just above absolute zero, where all cellular activity ceases, it is less than ideal.

Without the greater gift of the Holy Ghost, the real problem in the world is that in their efforts to clarify their consideration of Christ, even earnest seekers of truth are only "multiplying mirrors and studying angles without increasing the light." What is really needed is a flood of luminosity "that would not only replace the darkness, but would also illuminate elements and principles that, heretofore, had been only dimly perceived." (See B.H. Roberts, "The Truth, The Way, The Life", p. 263).

If we attempt to increase the light by playing the angles, we might be able to see a bit more clearly, but still, many basic principles will remain only dimly perceived. The problem is that when we attempt to manipulate the Light of Christ, we are only spinning our wheels. What is really needed is more light! Heavenly Father, with the enthusiastic participation of the Holy Ghost, and the approbation of Jesus Christ, has orchestrated the Restoration in order to address the problem of chronic gloominess in the world. He wants us to enjoy the scenic areas He has created especially for us. Hence, the Savior appeared to Joseph Smith in the Sacred Grove as "the light which shineth in darkness." (D&C 11:11).

Scenic Byway

When the
Lord created the
earth, He pronounced
it "Good." (Genesis 1:10).
When He looked over all of
His creations at the end of the
sixth day, He pronounced
His work "Very Good."
(Genesis 1:31).

With a stroke of genius, Heavenly Father created our eyes, not only that we might see clearly, and discern between good and evil, but also that we might see with vibrancy every color of an eternal spectrum.

Our vision resonates with intrinsic light that is not a reaction to pigments and dyes. The light of the Spirit responds to our divine nature with a vibrancy, vitality, and vivacity that can only fade if we neglect to nurture it.

The scenic Highways and Byways of Life introduce us to a cornucopia of color. Psychophysicists tell us that the human eye can distinguish around 10 million different shades, which is really quite remarkable, since there are only three primary colors in the visible light spectrum (red, green, and blue). Isaac Newton, who was the first to use a prism to separate white light (at wavelengths between 390 – 700 nm) into its individual colors, divided the spectrum into seven named colors (red, orange, yellow, green, blue, indigo, and violet).

In general, though, the color red calls us to action, and reminds us that the Savior trod the winepress alone. Orange is a warning to take care that we conform our lives to the Lord's design. Yellow encourages us to seek the light that is gathering in the east. Green brings to mind the power of envy, our requirement to observe and keep the 10th commandment, and satisfaction with the cards in the hand that God has dealt us. Blue reminds us to mourn with those that mourn, and to comfort those that stand in need of comfort. Indigo is a color whose depth and brightness represent the profundity of the Gospel, and its ability to illuminate truth wherever it may be found. Violet is the color of amethyst, lavender and beautyberries, and reminds us of the garlands festooning the walls of the celestial city of God. (See Revelation 21:20).

Grey (black and white) is associated with neutrality, conformity, uncertainty, and indifference. It prompts us to choose whom we will serve and encourages us to stand on the Lord's side. Purple (red and blue) urges us to remember the royal robes of Christ our King. Black (blue, red, and yellow) underscores the necessity of opposition that paves the way for our progression. White (red, orange, yellow, green, blue, indigo and violet) solemnly suggests the totality of the ordinances of the priesthood, our temple covenants, the brotherhood of man, and the purity of the

Spirit, all of which are necessary if we are to regain the glory of our former home.

From ultraviolet to infrared, the pattern and design of color along the Scenic Highways and Byways of Life will resonate with radiation from a spectrum that can only be seen with eyes that have been touched by the hand of God. If we were able to break down that energy with a spiritual prism, we would look beyond the limited horizon of our sight and behold the visions of eternity. "By the power of the Spirit our eyes (would be) opened and our understandings (would be) enlightened, so as to see and understand the things of God." (D&C 76:12). We would see before us "all things bright and beautiful, all creatures great and small, and all things wise and wonderful", and we would know that "the Lord God made them all." (Cecil Francis Alexander).

When Jesus Christ created our world, He anticipated our movement through mortality by generously sprinkling Scenic Byways everywhere we would turn. (See Mosiah 3:8, & Moses 2:1). He hoped that, by doing so, our hearts would swell with gratitude, and wonderful things would happen.

Good would outweigh evil. Love would overpower jealousy, hate, and prejudice. Light would drive out darkness and bats. Knowledge would banish ignorance. Humility would displace pride. Courtesy would overwhelm ill manners. Appreciation would overcome thanklessness. Abundance would supersede poverty. Well-being would replace weakness. Simplicity would overshadow perplexity. Harmony would supplant discord. Faith would conquer fear. Hope would cast out despair. Charity would subdue selfishness. Joy would depose unhappiness, sadness, dejection, and misery. Confidence would be substituted for timidity. Certainty would dethrone bewilderment. Assurance would unseat discouragement and even despair.

The scenic beauty of the Highways and Byways of Life has a way of opening our eyes to the wonders of this world, as though seeing them for the first time.

School Bus Stop Ahead

The
Gospel is a
schoolmaster, to
bring us to Christ,
which is why we have
been blessed to have so
many School Bus Stops
along the Highways
and Byways of
Life.

The blueprints of life's learning laboratory diagram safe passage along its Highways and Byways. It core curriculum documents potential perils and pitfalls, charts recommended routes that leads to refuge, maps out success strategies for abundant living, and measures our progress on the pathway to perfection. The elements of this roadmap are the principles and doctrines of The Plan of Salvation. They are similar to the World Wide Web that, for access, requires only computer literacy, an I.P. address with a network, and relevant hardware and software. The mainframe of The Plan must exist somewhere, although its exact location is very hazy. A best guess is that it is in the neighborhood of Kolob. The storage of its data certainly exceeds that of the internet, which in 2019 was estimated to be in the neighborhood of 1,200 petabytes. That is 1.2 million terabytes, or 1.2 billion gigabytes.

It is the mind-boggling storage and retrieval capacity of The Plan that has the potential to order our chaotic world, to bless us with clarity rather than confusion, to teach us fluency in the language of the Spirit, and to educate those who are functionally illiterate so that they, too, might be mesmerized by the power of the lessons to be learned, as we move along on the Highways and Byways of Life.

Those who utilize the principles of The Plan to guide them, as they travel along, learn by personal experience that the greatest miracle is not technology, or even the raising of the physically dead, but the healing of the spiritually sick. It is with His guidance and direction that our Heavenly Father prepares us to receive eternal life. With them, our eyes are opened, our vision is perfected, and our sight is lifted above artificial horizons and life's limitations. As we move along, we are rewarded, now and then, with a tantalizing glimpse of eternity, where our future lies.

As Q told Captain Jean Luc Picard, whose highway was interstellar: "You just don't get it, do you? The trial never ends. We wanted to see if you had the ability to expand your mind and your horizons, and for one brief moment, you did. For one fraction of a second, you were open to options you had never considered. That is the exploration that awaits you. Not mapping stars and studying nebulae, but charting the unknown possibilities of existence." ("Star Trek: The Next Generation").

School Zone

As
we journey
upon the Highways
and Byways of Life,
we will encounter school
zone after school zone, where
we will slow down, and often stop,
for much-needed enlightenment. But
we are also as the day-old child,
of whom the poet wrote.

"My day old child lay in my arms. With my lips against his ear, I whispered strongly, 'How I wish, I wish that you could hear. I've a hundred wonderful things to say. (A tiny cough and a nod). Hurry, hurry, hurry and grow, so I can tell you about God.' My day-old baby's mouth was still, and my words only tickled his ear. But a kind of a light passed through his eyes, and I saw this thought appear: 'How I wish I had a voice, and words. I've a hundred things to say. Before I forget, I'd tell you of God. I only left Him yesterday.'" (Carol Lynn Pearson, "Day Old Child").

Accepting the challenge to expand our minds and our horizons in order to plumb the unknown possibilities of existence forces us to ask ourselves if we have embraced the moral element of responsibility to goes hand in hand with knowledge? Do we have the spiritual and intellectual maturity to handle knowledge with accountability? When we dare to grapple with these interrogatives, we come to an epiphany, as we determine to do our best to be righteous stewards. It was with this in mind that Joshua asked Israel: "Choose you this day whom ye will serve." (Joshua 24:15).

We realize that we have been given the privilege to be bathed in an innervating vitality, and to be empowered with an otherworldly serenity, as we struggle to keep our heads above water in the agar of experience into which we have been cast; the petri dish of mortality, if you will. As Bagheera, the powerfully built black panther confided to Mowgli the man-cub, in "The Jungle Book": "I had never seen the jungle. They fed me behind bars from an iron pan until one night I felt that I was Bagheera the Panther, and no man's plaything, and I broke the lock with one blow of my paw, and I came away." (Rudyard Kipling).

GDOT
Georgia Department of Transportation

Secure Your Load

The
righteous
are confident
that the burdens
that have been placed
upon their shoulders will
not shift, because they have
been fastened with the strong
cords of commitment, bound with
the sturdy harness of covenants,
and secured with the sure
ties of consecration.

The drag of uncertainty, the heavy weight of indecision, and the soul-compromising cancer of indiscretion, will slow down the unrighteous who have not secured their load. The friction of sin grating against the strait and narrow way will unnecessarily heat up its smooth cobblestones, making it uncomfortable for the unrepentant to continue along that path. The righteous, on the other hand, although they may awaken to calm seas and fair weather, take note of a red sky at morning. They do not want to find themselves gliding smoothly and effortlessly through life, because by sad experience they have discovered that, when they do so, they are generally going downhill. Instead, they secure their load. They want to be steadily improving, and moving upward against ever-present obstacles, as they encounter and conquer opposition.

The righteous dream big. They nurture spirituality. They are known as persons of character, with clearly defined and realistic goals. They do not procrastinate, but accept responsibility. They do what they love to do, establish priorities, and stick with them. They are understanding, and consciously choose habit patterns that are based on correct principles. They have single-minded concentration when the Spirit has dictated a specific course of action, but in other circumstances they remain flexible in their approach to problem-solving. They never consider the possibility of failure. They are honest and dedicated to service. They are not managers, but are leaders who recognize and act upon the switch-points in their lives. They love to work and are dependable. They have a clear vision of who they are, and they persist at tasks until they succeed. They seize the moment. They are unified and are teachers and mentors. They know that it can get bumpy as they travel, day by day, along the Highways and Byways of Life, and so they take the time to Secure their Load before venturing out.

See Tracks? Think Train

When, on the Highways and Byways of Life, we hear hoofbeats, we think horses. But it might just be a herd of zebras that is approaching.

Boyd K. Packer was once asked, "What is the future of the Lamanites in the Church?" His immediate response was: "I cannot answer that question. We have no '-ites' in The Church." In contemporary terms, we could say the same thing about people or organizations that attempt to artificially segregate people into classes, cultures, racial stereotypes, political persuasions, economic divisions, and the like, in particular if they do so to promote a private agenda.

We remember the conditions among the people of Zarahemla who had been stripped of the pride and contention that describe and define the distinctions created by anarchistic individuals with hidden agendas: "There were no robbers, nor murderers, neither were there Lamanites, nor any manner of -ites; but they were in one, the children of Christ, and heirs to the kingdom of God." (4 Nephi 1:17).

The Apostle Paul similarly described the Ephesians: "Now therefore ye are no more strangers and foreigners, but fellowcitizens with the saints, and of the household of God." (Ephesians 2:19). They were members of one of the seven churches of Asia, and might have considered themselves the privileged few of an "exclusive ecclesiastical country club." (Neal A. Maxwell). He urged them to avoid applying complimentary labels to themselves while talking about others disparagingly.

Paul was saying to the Ephesians that, should foreigners from Corinth, Philippi, or Colossi arrive in Ephesus, they should not thought of as strangers, but should rather be recognized as part of a cooperative community, and that, in their thinking, the body of the Church should be characterized as a household that lived with the bonds of full faith and fellowship.

On the Highways and Byways of Life, our fellow travelers who respond to the invitation to come unto Christ come out of the world, and leave "the loneliness and estrangement of a fallen creation and enter the realm of divine experience. They forsake the orphanage of spiritual alienation and are received into the family and household of the Lord Jesus Christ. They leave the ranks of the nameless and take upon them the blessed name of Jesus Christ. They are Christians. Through their Master, they become, in time, joint heirs to all that the Father has." (Robert L. Millet, et. al., "Doctrinal Commentary on The Book of Mormon", 4:202).

When we see train tracks running alongside the Highways and Byways of Life, we must take are that we do not immediately jump to conclusions that might not be supported by the facts. We must not apply labels to others that artificially categorize or compartmentalize them, segregate them from the blessings of the Gospel, limit their potential, demean their status as children of our Heavenly Father, or communicate mistrust, misunderstanding, or even worse, contempt.

Is there really a palpable, perceptible difference between the prince and pauper, those who bask in the limelight and those who hug the shadows, member and non-member, active and inactive individual, or single, divorced, widowed, and married people? Are saints and sinners so very different?

The Lord God "inviteth them all to come unto him and partake of his goodness; and he denieth none that come unto him, black and white, bond and free, male and female; and he remembereth the heathen; and all are alike unto God, both Jew and Gentile." (2 Nephi 26:33). Nephi could not have put it more emphatically than to say that both Jew and Gentile are the same in the eyes of our Heavenly Father, for the Jews of his day were almost fanatically obsessed with their status as the Chosen People of God. This verse gives notice to all, across centuries of prejudice, mistrust, and discrimination, that God is indeed no respecter of persons, but rather that it is righteousness alone that is important to Him. (D&C 38:16, see Ephesians 6:9).

More particularly, members living in the United States need to remember that organizations like Black Lives Matter and ANTIFA do not exit in heaven. Nor do liberals or conservatives or activists of any kind. Nor, for that matter, does the United States of America. (The expression: "Children of God" appears 369 times in the scriptures, however. That is a group that is worthy of our membership).

Severe Weather Shelter

Lightning is
a "striking" example
of the storm of God, and
we are reminded of Him each
time we witness its blinding flash
accompanied by a resounding clap
of thunder. Those of us "who hath
seen any or the least of these
hath seen God moving in
his majesty and power."
(D&C 88:47).

That seething energy envelops the earth and turns it into a fiery hot cauldron. There are estimated to be around 2,000 lightning storms raging across the face of the earth at any given time, contributing to over 100 ground strikes per second. The air around these can reach a temperature 3 times hotter than the surface of the sun. The estimated peak power of a single bolt can be 1,000 Giga Watts (one thousand million watts). The total energy pent up and often released in a single large thunderstorm has been compared to that which would meet the needs of the United States for 20 minutes.

These are impressive statistics, but lightning is just a whisper of the power and influence of the Holy Ghost. To provide ancient Israel with a constant reminder of YHWH, a fire was kept burning upon the altar in the temple. (See Leviticus 6:13). When Moses climbed Sinai, "the angel of the Lord appeared unto him in a flame of fire out of the midst of a bush: and he looked, and, behold, the bush burned with fire, and the bush was not consumed." (Exodus 3:2). Channukah, the Jewish Festival of Light, commemorates the miracle in the temple when the candles of the Menorah burned for eight days, after being filled with only enough oil to last for one.

The recurring miracle, however, is not our witness of thunderstorms, or of burning bushes, or of lamps that do not fail, but that "truth shineth!" (D&C 88:7). Even the least among us can discern between truth and its dark counterpart, because only the former has an intrinsic glow and an enduring quality. It lasts forever, for "intelligence, or the light of truth, was not created or made, neither indeed can be." (D&C 93:29).

The physical manifestations of severe weather that we encounter along the Highways and Byways of Life remind us of the power of God, for it is He Who "maketh lightnings." (Psalms 135:7). It is His voice that is the thunder in the heavens, and it is His lightning that streaks across the sky and causes the earth to tremble and shake. (See Psalms 77:18). Perhaps lightning was created by the hand of God as a type and a shadow, for it "cometh out of the east, and shineth even unto the west. So shall also the coming of the Son of man be." (Matthew 24:27).

Share The Road

Heavenly Father's
Plan of Happiness is within the
reach of every one of us, no matter
what our cultural, economic, political,
social or theological circumstances
might be. On the Highways and
Byways of Life, we all
Share The Road.

The pavement of The Plan is strengthened by the rebar of the scriptures, buttressed by Gospel doctrine, and reinforced by principles that testify of its depth. We can add pitifully little to the integrity of the roadbed, no matter that we are princes or paupers, rich or poor, humble or proud, strong or weak, tall or short, happy or sad, fat or thin, good or evil, or saints or sinners.

When we see so many, from so many different walks of life, sharing the road, we find ourselves swept up through the miracle of the infinite, continuing, uninterrupted, unspoiled, uncorrupted, enduring, unfathomable and immeasurable grace of God that is embodied within the Atonement, and we are swallowed up in joy, "even to the exhausting of (our) strength." (Alma 27:17).

With that epiphany, our hearts will "brim with joy." (Alma

26:11). God's Perfect Plan is designed to save all of His children in His Celestial Kingdom! (See Dallin Oaks, C.R., 4/2019). His mission statement reveals that His carefully crafted Plan is not just a hobby; it is the very real work to which He gives His undivided attention. (See Moses 1:39). His Plan was not just designed so that we might live forever. It was created to teach us how to live now, how to enjoy the dominion He enjoys, how to create a heaven on earth, and how to use the tools He has provided, that we might have a hope of eternal life even as we engage humanity and Share The Road as we travel the Highways and Byways of life.

His perfect Plan has the depth, breadth, majesty, and capacity to encircle all of His children within His warm embrace. As the poet wrote: "He scribed a circle that drew me out. Heretic, rebel, a thing to flout! But love and I had the will to win. We scribed a circle that drew him in." (Edwin Markham). Surely, the example of the Savior's love teaches that this is exactly what He did during his ministry.

After the conclusion of the War in Heaven, when God pronounced His subsequent creations as "good" He said that His crowning achievement, "us", was, in fact, "very good." (Moses 2:4, 10, 12, 18, 21, 25 & 31). The earthly environment He had fashioned for our enjoyment was ideally suited to nurture not only the favored "first part" of His creations, but also the "second" part, and perhaps, for all we know, even the "third" part.

The Lord's Atonement, after all, is the keystone of a Plan that was conceived from before the foundation of the world to be perfect in its redemptive capacity. We can scarcely comprehend its infinite and eternal scope, and how directly influences even our Father's children who have not known Christ. As Paul said to those who had gathered to hear him preach on Mars Hill: "As I passed by, and beheld your devotions, I found an altar with this inscription, 'To the Unknown God.' Whom therefore ye ignorantly worship,' him declare I unto you." (Acts 17:23).

Not all have been as fortunate as Jacob, who "knew of Christ, and ... had a hope of his glory many hundred years before his coming." (Jacob 4:4). With its breathtaking reconciliation of Justice and Mercy within the matrix of free will, the Atonement makes The Plan perfect, for the men and women of Athens in Paul's day, as well as for the 7.8 billion souls who travel the Highways and Byways of Life in ours. It seems reasonable that it would allow the worst of us to work out our salvation and earn the privilege, as prodigal sons and daughters of God, to rejoin His household in full fellowship, with all the rights and privileges one would expect, following the reformation of errant behavior. Is this not what the principle of repentance is all about? After all, there is so much good in the worst of us, and so much bad in the best of us, that it hardly behooves any of us to talk about the rest of us.

Sharp Curves

> The sharp curves that we
> all encounter all along the
> Highways and Byways of Life
> remind us of a land before
> time, when the physical and
> spiritual properties of light
> and darkness contributed
> to a division among the
> children of God, that
> culminated in a
> war in heaven.

We can almost hear the clash as opposing ideologies grated against each other, as "Michael and his angels fought against the dragon, and the dragon and his angels fought against Michael." (J.S.T. Revelation 12:6). Nephi wrote of the eternal consequences of that conflict that centered around the Sharp Curves in the pathway leading to a correct understanding of The Plan of Salvation. "Our father also saw that the justice of God did also divide the wicked from the righteous; and the brightness thereof was like unto the brightness of a flaming fire, which ascendeth up unto God forever and ever, and hath no end." (1 Nephi 15:30).

During His mortal ministry, Christ was "the life and the light of the world (and) the word of truth and righteousness."

(Alma 38:9). He declared: "I am come a light into the world, that whosoever believeth on me should not abide in darkness." (John 12:46). Isaiah had prophetically declared that His glory would "kindle a burning like the burning of a fire." (Isaiah 10:16). David expressed the hope we all share, that he would be delivered from the jaws of death, so that he might "walk before God in the light of the living." (Psalms 56:13).

Without the influence of the Savior, and without the comfort of knowing that we have the guidance of the Holy Ghost upon which we can rely, "we wait for light, but behold obscurity; for brightness, but we walk in darkness. We grope for the wall like the blind ... as if we had no eyes: we stumble at noonday as in the night; we are in desolate places as dead men. We roar like bears, and mourn sore like doves: we look for judgment, but there is none; for salvation, but it is far off from us. For our transgressions are multiplied before (God), and our sins testify against us." (Isaiah 59:9-12).

In contrast, the light that is kindled by the Holy Ghost shows us the way to dwell within the secure envelope of the word of God. It is "a lamp unto (our) feet, and a light unto (our) path." (Psalms 119:105). God's bright and beautiful creations draw us closer to Him. "All creatures great and small. All things wise and wonderful. The Lord God made them all." (Cecil Francis Alexander).

SIDEWALK CLOSED

Sidewalk Closed

The sidewalk
that runs alongside
the Highways and Byways
of Life, as a general rule,
remains closed to the public.
There is no time for spectators
to take a leisurely stroll as a
respite from life's journey.
The Plan requires that
we remain actively
engaged.

"Motivation", Steven Covey taught, "is a fire from within." As the process of our conversion unfolds, our discipline urges us to be up and about and moving on the Highways and Byways of Life. We recognize the wisdom in the observation of Hans Christian Anderson, who said our lives are fairy tales waiting to be written by the hand of God." A number of the chapters in the story of our lives have already been set to paper, and we don't know how many yet remain to be written. But we do know this: although God has set an admittedly high standard, we must follow the course He has established. (The word "follow" appears 312 times in the scriptures). We cannot start over and make a new beginning, but we can begin now and make a new ending. It is time for us to engage ourselves in writing our story.

As the seasons of our lives unfold, we learn that "Life is a sheet of paper white, where each of us may write a line or two, and then comes night. Greatly begin! If thou hast time for but a line, make that sublime. Not failure, but low aim, is crime." (James Russell Lowell).

Signal Ahead

When we
see a sign indicting
that there is a Signal Ahead,
we are reminded that there are
powers greater than ourselves that
influence the flow of traffic
along the Highways and
Byways of Life.

Jesus Christ is the Creator of those signals, and if we were to gaze up into the heavens, we would realize that He is also the Architect of the cosmos, including the "Pillars of Creation", elephant trunks of interstellar gas and dust in the Eagle Nebula, 7,000 light years from Earth. When we see their image that has been captured by the Hubble Space Telescope, we realize that anyone "who hath seen any or the least of" the trillions of stars in the universe, "hath seen God moving in His majesty and power." (D&C 88:47).

In an 1857 sermon entitled "The Condescension of Christ", London pastor Charles Spurgeon used the phrase to describe both the physical world and the force stemming from the divine that binds it all together. "Now wonder, ye angels", he wrote of the birth of Christ, "the Infinite has become an infant. He, upon whose shoulders the universe doth hang, nurses at his mother's breast; He who created all things and bears up the pillars of creation!"

And all the time, we thought the signals we see on the Highways and Byways of Life just regulated the flow of terrestrial traffic. It does pay to look up, every now and then, as did Ralph Waldo Emerson. He mused that when we "have seen the rising moon break out of the clouds at midnight, we have been present like an archangel at the creation of light and of the world." He also wrote that "if the stars should appear but one night in a thousand years, how would men believe and adore, and preserve for many generations the remembrance of the city of God which had been shown?"

Signal Operation Changed

When Joseph Smith "saw a pillar
of light exactly over (his) head, above
the brightness of the sun (that) descended
gradually until it fell upon (him), the
world didn't realize it yet, but
everything had changed.
(J.S.H. 1:16).

Without light, life as we know it would not exist. It is in light that we carry out most of our activities. We even call them "daily" routines instead of "nightly" routines, and those who work in the dark in the hours just before dawn toil in the "graveyard shift."

Because of its beneficial physical characteristics, light is used as a symbol to powerful effect. When an idea explodes in our minds, it is as if a light bulb had turned on. Glimmers of truth enlighten us as they illuminate the dark recesses of our thoughts. When the equations of relativity jelled in his brain, Albert Einstein said of the experience: "A splendid light dawned on me." When we research a question, our focused efforts shed light on the problem. As we endure hardship, we are comforted because we can see the light at the end of the tunnel. When stark reality sets in, our challenges seem less daunting in the light of day. As the pop tune suggests, a special someone has the power to light up our lives.

In the scriptures, light has been used as a symbol of Jesus Christ, as well as of the Holy Ghost At the Feast of Tabernacles commemorating the Lord's blessings to the children of Israel during their travels in the wilderness, the flames from four enormous candelabra that illuminated the temple could be seen throughout Jerusalem. How appropriate that it was in this setting that Jesus announced: "I am the light of the world: he that followeth me shall not walk in darkness, but shall have the light of life." (John 8:12).

Jesus is "the light of truth, which truth shineth. This is the Light of Christ. As also he is in the sun, and the light of the sun, and the power thereof by which it was made. As also he is in the moon, and is the light of the moon, and the power thereof by which it was made. As also the light of the stars, and the power thereof by which they were made. And the earth also, and the power thereof, even the earth upon which you stand. And the light which shineth, which giveth you light, is through him who enlighteneth your eyes, which is the same light that quickeneth your understandings, Which light proceedeth forth from the presence of God to fill the immensity of space — The light which is in all things, which giveth life to all things, which is the law by which all things are governed, even the power of God who sitteth upon his throne, who is in the bosom of eternity, who is in the midst of all things." (D&C 88:6-13).

As we strive to be like Jesus, we reflect His light and become, with Him, "the light of the world." (Matthew 5:14). It is in this sense that the Savior urged: "Let your light so shine before men, that they may see your good works and glorify your Father which is in heaven." (Matthew 5:16). "People are like stained glass windows. They sparkle and shine when the sun is out, but when the darkness sets in their true beauty is revealed only if there is a light from within." (Elizabeth Kubler-Ross). It is in this sense that with the Restoration of the Gospel, the Signal Operation has Changed, and with the help of the Holy Ghost, we can light the world.

Slight Curve Ahead

Within the
United States of America,
every four years there is a Slight
Curve Ahead, as voters recalibrate,
hopefully with greater precision, what
Alexander Hamilton described as the
"Grand Experiment in Democracy."
("Federalist Paper #9").

We would do well to remember that the Golden Age of Greece was founded upon common culture, and it failed. Rome was founded upon law, and it failed. Alexander the Great founded his empire upon power, and it also failed. America was founded upon a basis of religion and education, and it remains to be seen what its destiny will be.

Consider this: Twenty-three of the first twenty-four universities in America were founded by religious organizations. During America's first 150 years, churches provided nearly all the institutions of higher learning, producing leaders of thought and champions of liberty who enriched the republic. Thomas Jefferson was an alumnus of William and Mary, and James Madison of Princeton. Alexander Hamilton was an alumnus of what is now Columbia University.

It is interesting to note that all but eight of the fifty-five who signed the Declaration of Independence, and most of those who wrote the Constitution, were nurtured by the atmosphere of church-supported institutions of higher learning. Jefferson declared that people cannot be ignorant and remain free. The founding of the University of Virginia was the crowning achievement of his life.

Benjamin Franklin was proud to have been the founder of the University of Pennsylvania. George Washington left a $50,000 bequest to further higher education, and Washington and Lee University was the recipient of that legacy.

The early leaders of church and state in America were the products of schools begun by orthodox Christianity. Sixteen of the first eighteen Presidents of the United States were college graduates from church-related institutions of higher learning. Seven Chief Justices of the Supreme Court have been graduates of church-related universities.

If there is a Slight Curve Ahead on America's Highways and Byways, let us hope and pray that its citizens will have the moral backbone to elect to public office those who will not only champion freedom, but who will also acknowledge the hand of God in their affairs, and protect the religious freedoms of all citizens.

In the second decade of the Twenty First Century, it is trendy to trash not only our Founding Fathers, but also anyone whose public or private behavior has ever deviated from currently acceptable values or norms. But listen to what the cultural icons of our republic had to say about government, religion, and moral responsibility.

George Washington: "Whatever may be conceded to the influence of refined education on minds of peculiar structure, reason and experience both forbid us to expect that national morality can prevail in exclusion of religious principle."

Thomas Jefferson: "I shall need, too, the favor of that Being in whose hands we are, who led our forefathers, as Israel of old, from their native land, and planted them in a country flowing with all the necessaries and comforts of life." (Second Inaugural Address).

James Madison: "If angels were to govern men, neither external nor internal controls on government would be necessary."

Abraham Lincoln: "I am loath to close. We are not enemies, but friends. We must not be enemies. Though passion may have strained it must not break our bonds of affection. The mystic chords of memory, stretching from every battlefield and patriot grave to every living heart and hearthstone all over this broad land, will yet swell the chorus of the Union, when again touched, as surely they will be, by the better angels of our nature." (First Inaugural Address).

Harry S. Truman: "At this moment, I have in my heart a prayer. As I have assumed my duties, I humbly pray Almighty God, in the words of King Solomon, 'Give therefore Thy servant an understanding heart to judge Thy people, that I may discern between good and bad: for who is able to judge this Thy so great a people?' I ask only to be a good and faithful servant of my Lord and my people." (In his first address to Congress following the death of Franklin Delano Roosevelt).

Finally, John Winthrop, one of the founders of the Massachusetts Bay Colony: "The only way to avoid this shipwreck (that looms just around the Slight Curve Ahead) and to provide for our posterity is to do justly, to love mercy, and to walk humbly with our God. We must be knit together in this work as one; we must entertain each other in affection. We must delight in each other, to make others' condition our own, rejoice together, mourn together, labor, and suffer together. For we must consider that we shall be as a city upon a hill, and the eyes of all people are upon us. If we deal falsely with our God in this work we have undertaken, and so cause Him to withdraw His present help from us, we shall be made a story and a by-word through the world. We shall shame the faces of many of God's worthy servants, and cause their prayers to be turned into curses upon us."

Slippery When Wet

> Heavenly Father
> never said it would be
> easy, but He has assured
> us that our struggles
> would be well
> worth it.

It is a marvelous thing to see how the Gospel helps us to handle the challenges we face on the Highways and Byways of Life. We can feel the growth occurring almost on a daily basis. We must never think that our weaknesses are imperfections; rather, they are as stepping-stones that have been strategically placed, according to God's divine design, to help us to safely negotiate the rapids of life, for they are Slippery When Wet. When God created us, He pronounced us good, with an extra measure of resolve to see things through to their successful conclusion, or in the case of challenges, to their resolution based on Gospel principles.

The poet wrote: Why is it whenever I reach for the sky to climb aboard Cloud Nine, it evaporates and rains upon my dreams? Is it a matter of science, or simply a matter of fact, that not even a cloud with a silver lining can hold the weight of our dreams without some precipitation? I think I've found the answer to this dilemma. Keep on reaching for the sky, but don't forget your umbrella. (Susan Stephenson, "Cloud Nine").

SLOW

DRIVE AS IF YOUR KIDS WERE PLAYING ON THIS STREET

Slow

We need to move along the
Highways and Byways of
Life with responsibility,
as if our own kids
were playing on
the street.

Knowing what we do about the War in Heaven, it is no wonder that our youth are so zealous regarding the "exercise" of their agency.

It seems as if they are always chasing a ball, running to meet a friend, or riding their bike or scooter down the Highways and Byways of Life. As we watch them play, we realize that they were among the most valiant spirits in the pre-earth existence, and that during the ideological War in Heaven, which was fought by Lucifer for the control of our minds, they were passionate in the defense of self-determination.

During that conflict, the principle of moral agency, free will, or freedom of expression, prevailed and was adopted into The Plan of Salvation as its lynchpin. When the victorious spirits came to the earth clothed in bodies of flesh and bone, they did so with a passion for the freedom to choose their own destiny. Therefore, when those embodied spirits are controlled by compulsion, "in any degree of unrighteousness", it is ingrained within their nature to resist. Once again, we see at work the principle of opposition in all things.

It is helpful to understand why our youth feel as fervently as they do, and to be very cautious when questions arise that involve the exercise of moral agency. We need to be slow in our judgement, and quick to afterwards show an increase in love. At the same time, our youth must be taught to rely upon the powerful influence of the Holy Ghost, Who will help them to continue the pattern of correct choices that they initiated as pre-mortal spirits.

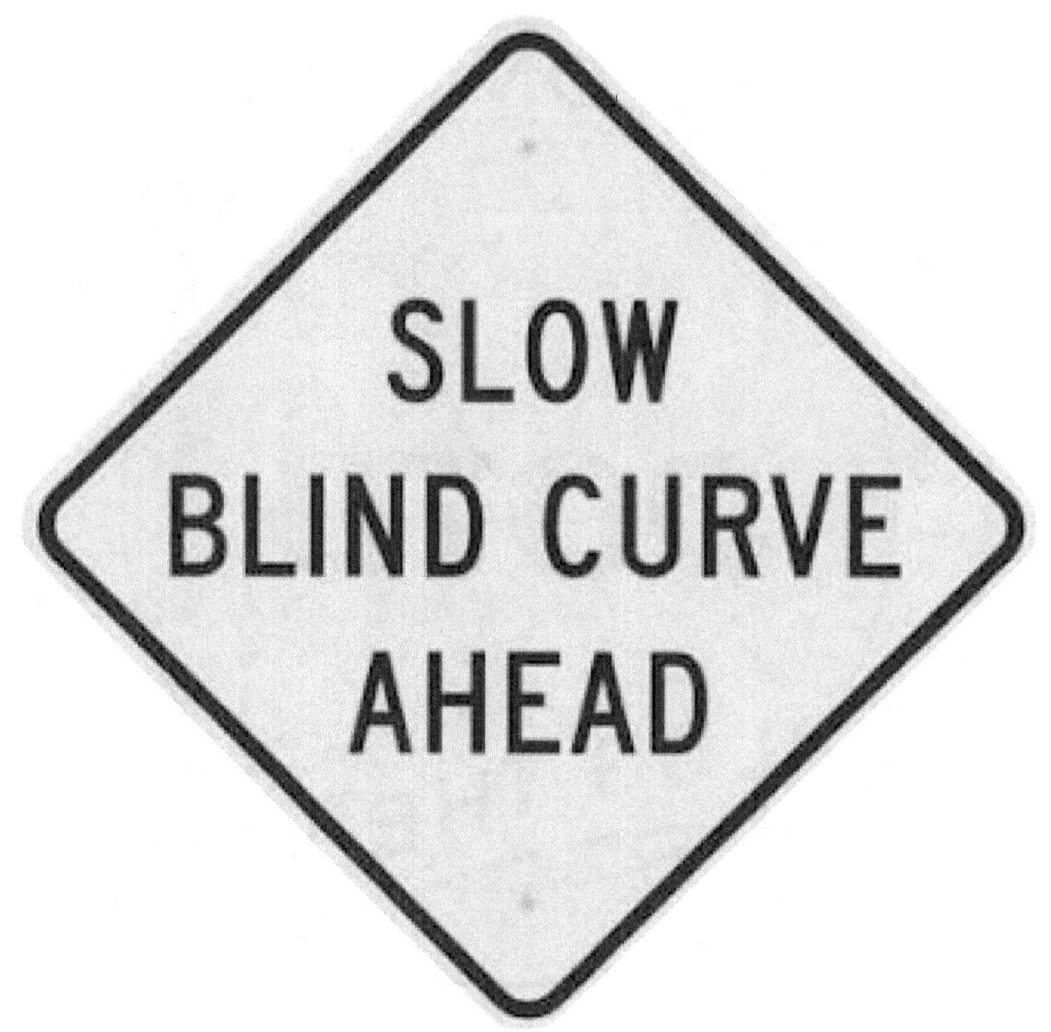

Slow: Blind Curve Ahead

The
Savior is
able to see the
Blind Curves Ahead;
He is "Alpha and Omega,
the beginning and the ending,
the Lord, who is, and who was, and
who is to come, the Almighty."
(J.S.T. Revelation 1:8).

Without the reassuring sense of stability that is provided by the Gospel, the Blind Curves Ahead can deal us a hand that leaves us a day late and a dollar short. If we attempt to negotiate the twists and turns that are built into the blueprint of the Highways and Byways of Life without our Master Navigator at the helm to guide us, we will find ourselves repetitively confronted by a conundrum of cosmic proportion. This must be the inexorable result of our failure to focus on an upward reach that is generated by our innate desire, capacity, and discipline to reach out and embrace the guiding hand of God. Each time we are caught unawares, the shock of confrontation with the Blind Curves that lie in our path will leave us gasping for a breath of celestial air.

Without the illumination that is provided by the headlamp

of Christ along the Highways and Byways of Life , we are doomed to suffer in a shadowy world where we will only experience illusions and caricatures of reality. When, on our own, we try to negotiate the convolutions that have been designed to build character , the discrepancy between what could have been His direction and our marginalized behavior can become so great that our short-lived pleasure in doing it our way and going it alone will evaporate as the morning dew in the full light of day.

Sooner or later, when this disparity becomes so great that it reaches "critical mass", a requisite readjustment will tear down the defensive façade that we have created, to allow the cultivation of a more nurturing lifestyle only made possible by a recommitment to reconciliation; to obedience to the foundation principles of The Plan.

These guiding lights will not only warn us of the impending dangers that lies ahead, but they will also illuminate the road map that allows us to safely move past whatever demons lie in wait along the curves in the road, so that we can resume our journey on the open roads of the Highways and Byways of Life.

NEBRASKA

Good Life. Great Journey.

DEPARTMENT OF TRANSPORTATION

SLOW

CONSTRUCTION AHEAD

PROCEED WITH EXTREME CAUTION

Slow: Construction Ahead

Each
of our lives
is a work in
progress.

The Savior is more interested in building our character than He is in anything else. That undertaking will be a long and slow process of growth. The attainment of our spiritual maturity will be a progressive development, until "we all come in the unity of the faith, and of the knowledge of the Son of God, unto a perfect man, unto the measure of the stature of the fulness of Christ." (Ephesians 4:13).

The Atonement stacks the deck in our favor, during that construction process. "The first condition of happiness", taught David O. McKay, "is a clear conscience." In medical terms, before an abrasion can heal, it has to be clean. Anyone who has had a physician vigorously scrub out an ugly wound knows how carefully and thoroughly the task must be accomplished before sterile dressings may be applied and the healing process begins. The same principle applies during the fabrication of God's holy temples. (See 1 Corinthians 6:19).

There is no room for dry rot and there can be no skeletons lurking in the closet. We cannot superficially whitewash our sins to cover them up. The Savior described the Scribes and Pharisees as hypocrites, for they were "like unto whited sepulchres, which indeed appear beautiful outward, but are within full of dead men's bones, and of all uncleanliness." (Matthew 23:27).

If we pay close attention to detail during the construction of our holy temples, we will grow in stature until we have developed both the image and likeness of our Heavenly Father. As we pour the footings and the foundation walls, again during framing, and even while finish work is being performed, we will fail again and again in our efforts. This creates a problem because "no unclean thing can dwell with God", and yet it seems to be our nature to repeatedly deviate from His blueprints. Unfortunately, sin will stop our progress, as surely as would an OSHA safety violation. God, however, provided the principle of repentance, together with the Atonement of our Savior, so that we may yet become holy, even a building fitly framed. Therefore, we are commanded, "All men, everywhere, must repent." (Moses 6:57).

SLOW DOWN!

Slow Down!

All things
should be done
"in wisdom and order;
for it is not requisite that a
man should run faster than he
has strength. And again, it is
expedient that he should be
diligent, that thereby he
might win the prize."
(Mosiah 4:27).

Nor should we turn to the arm of flesh to give us a boost of telestial horsepower. When God measures us, He does not put the tape around our heads, or our biceps, or our quadriceps, but around our hearts.

"Great and marvelous are the works of the Lord", Jacob exclaimed. "How unsearchable are the depths of the mysteries of him; and it is impossible that man should find out all his ways. And no man knoweth of his ways save it be revealed unto him." (Jacob 4:8). "O the vainness, and the frailties, and the foolishness of men!" wrote Lehi. For "when the are learned, they think they are wise" and they suppose "they know of themselves, wherefore, their wisdom is foolishness and it profiteth them not." (2 Nephi 9:28-29).

As Paul cautioned the Colossian Saints: "Beware lest any

man spoil you through philosophy and vain deceit, after the tradition of men, after the rudiments of the world." (Colossians 2:8). For "the race is not to the swift, nor the battle to the strong." (Ecclesiastes 9:11).

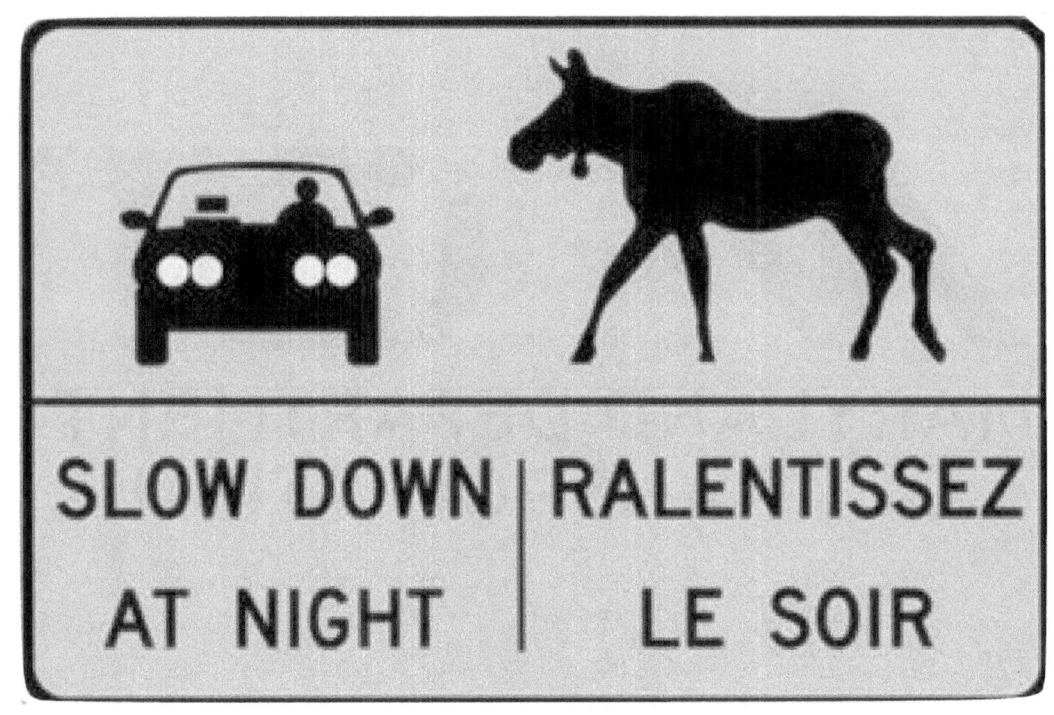

Slow Down At Night

There is wisdom in the admonition: "Retire to thy bed early." Each evening, we have the opportunity to ratchet down the hectic pace of our lives, that we might stop and smell the roses that have been carefully planted and lovingly cultivated by our Father in Heaven along our path of progress.

The evening hours are a good time to contemplate the word of God and to pause to pray. We can slow down our minds and free ourselves from the cares and concerns of the world. When we pick up our well-worn scriptures, the solemnities of eternity illuminate our minds, and when questions arise, we pray for understanding. We keep writing materials handy, knowing that reading will be an activity that stimulates the germination of ideas or original thoughts to which we will want to turn our attention. We read slowly.

We welcome the opportunity to engage in a study that is not a race. We don't have to finish a prescribed number of chapters or verses in an evening. If we like, we can spend hours pondering a single chapter or verse. We can read topically if we want to. We can interrupt our scripture study to find out what the prophets have said about the same subjects. As we memorize favorite passages, they bloom with hidden meanings we hadn't been aware of, and from time to time relevant life experiences pop into our minds, just when we need them the most to validate our internalization of principles and doctrines.

Because we Slow Down At Night, we can ask questions as we read. We solicit the companionship of the Holy Ghost, and we recognize His illuminating influence as our minds are flooded with light. Evenings provide us with opportunities to take a break from our busy activities, so we can think about the relevance of the passages we are currently studying. There is time to pause to let our minds work on their application.

Perhaps Helen Keller, who found it difficult to distinguish day from night, may have said it best: "The thought that my dear Heavenly Father is always near, giving me abundantly of all those things which truly enrich life and make it sweet and beautiful, makes every deprivation seem of little moment compared with the countless blessings I enjoy." ("The Story of My Life").

SLOW DOWN

OBEY SPEED LIMIT

Slow Down Obey Speed Limit

Travel will flow
much more smoothly
along the Highways and
Byways of Life, if everyone
obeys posted speed limits
and other traffic laws.
Prophets help all of
us to learn the
rules of the
road.

Over 150 years ago, John Greenleaf Whittier spoke of these modern prophets who encourage us to Slow Down and Obey the Speed Limit as we travel the Highways and Byways of Life. He said: "I discovered the great secret of their success in making converts. They speak to a common feeling; they minister to a universal want. They speak a language of hope and promise to the weak, weary hearts, tossed and troubled, who have wandered from sect to sect, seeking in vain for the primal manifestations of the divine power." ("A Mormon Conventicle", p. 461).

Slow Down: Uncontrolled Intersection Ahead

It is precisely
because we experience
uncertainty as we negotiate the
Highways and Byways of Life, that
we need to slow down and take
a deep breath, before we act
with imprudence and do
something we might
later regret.

As we deal with the uncontrolled intersections that lie in our path, along the Highways and Byways of Life, we learn to manage them as we can, to let go of the things that are beyond our power to change, and to have the wisdom to know the difference between the two.

Sometimes, the mayhem that occurs at Uncontrolled Intersections makes us feel as if we are headed toward the precipice of destruction, and that there is nothing we can do to influence the inevitable outcome.

According to The Science and Security Board of The Bulletin of Atomic Scientists, it is now 11:55 p.m. on the

Doomsday Clock, which represents a countdown to global catastrophe. Since 1947, the Board, including 18 Nobel Laureates, has maintained the clock and pessimistically adjusted its hour and second hand closer and closer to the apocalyptic hour of midnight. With just five minutes left until the clock strikes twelve, we can be sure that the angels in heaven have already raised their swords, and are only waiting upon the Lord's command to let them fall. (See D&C 1:13).

With so little time left, what does prudence dictate that we do? How can we deal wit the Uncontrolled Intersections that loom large in our future? We could roll the dice on the assumption that heaven can, and will, wait. We could put the inevitable out of our minds and dull our senses with the narcotics of immediate gratification and the hope and expectation of deferred consequences.

The problem with these flawed perspectives is that they lead to faulty perception, impaired judgment, and unfortunate and unanticipated consequences. In real life, things will not end well if we throw caution to the wind, and eat, drink, and make merry. The older we get, the more we realize that heaven can't wait, because we are already living in eternity.

Both Newton and Einstein, who toyed with the equations defining the arrow of time, may have been on to something. One or both of them may have been right, or both could have been equally wrong. Time may be absolute, or it may be relative to its frame of reference, or it may be neither.

Maybe the Father, Son, and Holy Ghost are the only Ones Who can have it both ways, and Who can tinker with time without paying homage to the laws of physics. They may have even found a way to slow down the hectic pace of our lives, that we might avoid traumatic confrontations with the Uncontrolled Intersections that lie in our future.

In any event, we can be sure that Their learning style is the only one that is expansive enough to accommodate the concept of eternal progression viewed from a temporal perspective, Uncontrolled Intersections notwithstanding. If the space-time continuum is thought of as a spatial and temporal matrix conceived by God to allow us to be free agents, then the frightening monsters that lie before us may be nothing more than our own coping mechanisms to help us deal with the day-to-day minor emergencies of mortality. If these disturbances are distortions in the fabric of time and space, they will require mending to restore equilibrium in the cosmos. These repair processes take shape as the laws governing faith, repentance, forgiveness, mercy, justice, and atonement. More than most of us realize, these laws of the Gospel are fundamental to our living, moving, and being in the face of Uncontrolled Intersections on the Highways and Byways of Life.

Time and space are in perfect balance when they allow us to regroup, reassess, repent, and take purposeful action. Thanks to Heavenly Father's omniscience, the observable elements of time and space have been linked to the immaterial element of agency, to combine into a single clarifying creation that coalesces to give us a swift kick in our complacency. This brings us to the conclusion that heaven really can't wait for us to come to grips with an uncertain future.

That acknowledgement may be the unified field theory of purposeful action that is the guiding principle to which the Grail Knight was referring in the motion picture "Indiana Jones and The Last Crusade." When we realize that heaven can't wait, our Quest takes on its deserved sense of urgency, and compels us to be about our Father's business. (See Luke 2:49).

When these elements of The Plan operate in harmony, there is still plenty of wiggle room within which we may make choices about how we are going to deal with unpredictability on the road ahead. The Plan provides us with currency sufficient to satisfy our needs, but it also provides us with "mad-money" (another example of opposition popping up in the most unexpected times and places) that we might substitute for legal tender wads of counterfeit cash with which we may attempt to make late payments that has had interest tacked on for bad behavior.

Remember, God controls our lives, in the sense that He guides and blesses us, but He always gives us our agency. If we try to subvert the uncertainty principle of The Plan with futile efforts to gain, obtain, and retain blessings we do not deserve, our efforts will be destabilizing. Time will grind on, but if we have sown the wind, we will inevitably reap the whirlwind. Because Uncontrolled Intersections lie in our future, we can count on the fact that a storm is probably coming. It's time to slow down and take a deep cleansing breath of celestial air, to prepare ourselves for what will be the experiences of a lifetime.

SLOW DOWN

ONLY
YOU CAN
PREVENT
SPEED
BUMPS

Slow Down: Only You Can Prevent Speed Bumps

As Polonius says to Laertes: This, above all, to thine own self be true, and it must follow, as the night the day, thou canst not then be false to any man." ("Hamlet", Act 1, Scene 3). Sometimes, it seems, we can be our own worst enemy.

The Prophet Joseph Smith said that our salvation consists of our being placed beyond the power of our enemies, meaning the enemies of our progression, such as dishonesty, greediness, lying, immorality, and other Speed Bumps.

Before we embarked upon the Highways and Byways of Life, our Heavenly Father could have given us everything He has, to make our journey more pleasant, but He knew that the most important part of the experience would be to discover ourselves and develop a divine nature. We are reminded of Dag Hammarskjöld's observation: "The longest journey is the journey inward, for he who has chosen his destiny has started upon a quest for the source of his being."

What we are, the essence of character, we have to earn for ourselves, as we struggle to overcome adversity and gain self-mastery. To help us to do so, our Heavenly Father promised that He would bless us with covenants that have been specifically designed to help us to focus our efforts. If it were not possible to become as He is, these covenants would be unnecessary.

It gives us great comfort to know that as we pass each milepost on the Highways and Byways of Life, avoiding as best we can the speedbumps of life, we are never alone, and that with each step of the way, we draw closer to our heavenly home. Through the mists of time, we can almost see the warm glow of God's porch light that is a beacon of hope to our tired eyes, and that will remain burning in hopeful anticipation of our arrival at His doorstep.

SLOWER TRAFFIC KEEP RIGHT

Slower Traffic Keep Right

The Gospel of Jesus Christ
is adapted to the capacity of
the weakest of those who travel
along the Highways and Byways
of Life. No matter what our
circumstances may be, we
are on safe ground as
long as we Keep
to the Right.

Closely related to "Merge Right", to "Lane Ends – Merge Right", and to "Keep Right" is the caution that "Slower Traffic should Keep Right." The Gospel is tailored to suit our individual circumstances, and yet it can be collectively understood and is universally applicable. The miracle is that each one of us, as slowly or as quickly as our circumstances dictate, can take our understanding as far as our faculties allow us to go. (See Ecclesiastes 9:11).

Insofar as our capacity to make covenants with God is concerned, He "doeth nothing save it be plain unto (us); and he inviteth (us) all to come unto him and partake of his goodness; and he denieth none that come unto him ... and all are alike unto God." (2 Nephi 26:33).

SLOW

ROAD UNDER REPAIR

Slow: Road Under Repair

As
we travel
the Highways
and Byways of Life,
anyone who thinks that
bliss is normal is going to
waste a lot of time running
around shouting to no-one
in particular that he's
he's been robbed.

The fact is that the road ahead of us is under repair pretty much all of the time. "Most of our putts don't drop, most beef is tough, most of our children grow up to just be people, most successful marriages require a high degree of mutual toleration, and most jobs are more often dull than otherwise. Life is like an old-time rail journey, with delays, sidetracks, smoke, dust, cinders and jolts, interspersed only occasionally by beautiful vistas and thrilling burst of speed. The trick is to thank the Lord for letting us have the ride." (Jenkin Lloyd Jones, Editor of "The Tulsa Tribune").

Slow: Rough Road Ahead

As we persevere
along the Highways and
Byways of Life, we pray "that
we might toil, and not seek for
rest; that we might give and not
count the cost; that we might fight,
and not heed the wounds; and
that we might labor, and not
ask for any reward, save
that of knowing that
we do God's will."
(Loyola).

There may be Rough Roads Ahead of us on the Highways and Byways of Life. The ominous sign is that bureaucrats and career politicians have lost their sense of divine purpose, at the same time that the people whom they serve are past repentance. Today, the temporal and spiritual equilibrium of entire societies hangs in the balance. Heaven must be holding its collective breath while waiting upon the initiative of those who have been charged with the sacred responsibility to provide good examples, and to take the lead when it comes to repentance.

We read in the Old Testament, that after his encounter with the leviathan, Jonah went to Nineveh, in accordance with the Lord's instruction. It is presumed by historians to have been the greatest city of the ancient world, not to mention its most wicked. Its people and their practices struck terror in the hearts of its neighbors. They had a reputation for shedding innocent blood, and so Jonah cried unto the king, who was probably Shalmaneser III, "and said, yet forty days, and Nineveh shall be overthrown. So the people of Nineveh believed God, and proclaimed a fast, and put on sackcloth, from the greatest of them even to the least of them." They cried mightily unto God, and everyone turned from their evil ways, and from violence, saying "who can tell if God will ... turn away from His fierce anger, that we perish not? (Jonah 3:1-0).

Later, when Jonah, in unrighteous judgment, was wroth with God for having spared the city, he was taught a great lesson. God asked him: "And should not I spare Nineveh, that great city, wherein are more than six score thousand persons that cannot discern between their right hand and their left hand?" (Jonah 4:11). In other words, God asked Jonah, should He not spare those who cannot discern between right and wrong, and yet are anxious to comply when they are called to repentance?

A modern-day equivalent of Shalmaneser III is Abraham Lincoln, who issued a "Proclamation Appointing a National Fast Day" in response to the jolting reality of deteriorating conditions in the Union. (April 30, 1863). Knowing that Rough Roads lay Ahead, it reads: "Whereas, the Senate of the United States, devoutly recognizing the supreme authority and just government of Almighty God, in all the affairs of men and of nations, has, by a resolution, requested the President to designate and set apart a day for national prayer and humiliation. And whereas it is the duty of nations as well as of men, to own their dependence upon the overruling power of God, to confess their sins and transgressions, in humble sorrow, yet with assured hope that genuine repentance will lead to mercy and pardon; and to recognize the sublime truth, announced in the holy scriptures and proven by all history, that those nations only are blessed whose God is the Lord. And, insomuch as we know that, by His divine law, nations like individuals are subjected to punishments and chastisements in this world, may we not justly fear that the awful calamity of civil war, which now desolates the land, may be but a punishment, inflicted upon us, for our presumptuous sins, to the needful end of our national reformation as a whole people?

We have been the recipients of the choicest bounties of heaven. We have been preserved, these many years, in peace and prosperity. We have grown in numbers, wealth and power, as no other nation has ever grown. But we have forgotten God. We have forgotten the gracious hand which preserved us in peace and multiplied and enriched and strengthened us; and we have vainly imagined, in the deceitfulness of our hearts, that all these blessings were produced by some superior wisdom and virtue of our own. Intoxicated with unbroken success, we have become too self-sufficient to feel the necessity of redeeming and preserving grace, too proud to pray to the God that made us! It behooves us then, to humble ourselves before the offended Power, to confess our national sins, and to pray for clemency and forgiveness.

Now, therefore, in compliance with the request, and fully concurring in the views of the Senate, I do, by this my proclamation, designate and set apart Thursday, the 30th day of April, 1863, as a day of national humiliation, fasting and prayer. And I do hereby request all the people to abstain, on that day, from their ordinary secular pursuits, and to unite, at their several places of public worship and their respective homes, in keeping the day holy to the Lord, and devoted to the humble discharge of the religious duties proper to that solemn occasion.

All this being done, in sincerity and truth, let us then rest humbly in the hope authorized by the divine teachings, that the united cry of the nation will be heard on high, and answered with blessings, no less than the pardon of our national sins, and the restoration of our now divided and suffering country, to its former happy condition of unity and peace."

SLOW
VEHICLES
USE
RIGHT
LANE

140

Slow Vehicles Use Right Lane

Our
Father
in Heaven
has created a
Slow Vehicle Lane
on the Highways and
Byways of Life simply
because He knows
each one of us
so well.

That lane invites us to ease off on the gas pedal when we need to, in order to slow down so that we can smell the roses. We are truly blessed when we learn that life is hard by the yard, but a cinch by the inch. It is this lesson that allows each one of us to reach our reward in the due time of the Lord. (See 1 Nephi 14:26). It is not requisite that we run faster or labor more than we have strength, (see D&C 10:4 & Mosiah 4:27), for "life is a sheet of paper white, where each of us may write a line or two, and then comes night. Greatly begin. If thou hast time but for a line, make that sublime. Not failure, but low aim is crime." (James Russell Lowell).

If we feel that we are already past the point of no return our journey, and that we are beyond redemption, we need to remember that although it may be too late to write a new beginning to our life's story, it is never too late to slow down and Use the Right Lane, where we can regroup, recover, repent, and rewrite a new ending.

Smiles to Go Before We Sleep

Go forward in life with a twinkle in your eye, and a smile on your face, but with great and strong purpose in your heart."
(Gordon B. Hinckley).

The following is adapted from Dale Carnegie's "How to Win Friends, and Influence People."

When interacting with others, don't criticize, condemn, or complain. Be honest and sincere in your appreciation. Arouse in others an eager want. If you want them to like you, become genuinely interested in them. Remember that their name is to them the sweetest and most important sound that they could hear. Be a good listener and encourage others to talk about themselves. Steer the conversation in the direction of their interests. Help them, in sincerity, to feel that they are important in your estimation.

Remember that the only way to get the best in an argument is to avoid it in the first place. Show respect for the opinions of others, and never tell them that they are wrong. If you are wrong, however accept ownership and freely acknowledge it. Begin in a friendly way conversations that have the potential to cause friction. Give others the opportunity to say "Yes" to the points that you make, even if they strengthen your position. Let them do most of the talking. Help them to feel that the ideas you are sharing are their own. Honestly try to see things from their point of view. There are always two sides to an "argument."

Be sympathetic with their ideas and desires. Appeal to their nobler motives. If you need to throw down a challenge, clothe it in language to which they can relate. If you hope to change someone's opinion without giving offense or arousing resentment, begin with praise and honest appreciation. Talk about your own shortcomings first, if you feel you must be critical of others. Only indirectly call attention to mistakes or imperfections.

If you feel compelled to take command of the conversation, try to ask questions instead. Let the other person save face. Praise their behavior or communication skills. Give them a reputation to live up to. With encouragement, make perceived faults easy to correct. With positive reinforcement, make them happy to do the things you suggest.

We all have Smiles To Go Before We Sleep, and so, should we not "persevere and go on in so great a cause? Go forward and not backward. Courage ... and on, on to the victory! Let your hearts rejoice and be exceedingly glad. Let the earth break forth into singing ... Let the mountains shout for joy, and all ye valleys cry aloud ... Let the woods and all the trees of the field praise the Lord, and ye solid rocks weep for joy! And let the sun, moon, and the morning stars sing together ... and let the eternal creations declare His name forever and ever." (D&C 128:22-23).

Speed Cameras

"The book of life is
engraved in our bones and
sinews. Every thought, word, and
deed has an effect on the human
body; all these leave their marks
which can be read by Him who is
Eternal as easily as the words
in a book can be read."
(Bruce R. McConkie).

Along the Highways and Byways of Life, Speed Cameras are constantly documenting our progress, and their storage and retrieval capabilities are infinite.

"My father focuses heart-gripping flashes across the wall screen. Family slides. I am small, my brother is smaller, and my sister is smallest. Days now dead re-open like old storybooks from memory's heaped box. Pulling out pictures of cooking in Grandfather's Dutch oven; playing cheetah in our backyard monkey-jungle; being beautifully Easter-bested with my coat buttoned wrong; hugging a mommy minus grey hair. Soberly, I think of another Father, Who someday shall open my mind, and flash reeling remembering of every day's minute across my soul, across the heavens, and kindly ask me to narrate." (Lora Lyn Stucker, "New Era", 8/1973).

SPEED CHECKED BY RADAR

Speed Checked By Radar

As we plod along
the Highways and Byways of
Life, we sometimes stop to ask
ourselves: "Does God obey
the speed limit?"

"For those who attain the presence of God, nowhere is really out of His presence, and now is forever. As time is no more, likewise space will shrink irrevocably. For all we know, the speed of light may prove to be too slow to do some of what must be done." (Neal A. Maxwell, "Ensign", 6/1982).

Until then, we are constrained by the cosmic speed limit within the physical universe wherein the speed of light is always the same, regardless of the speed at which we may be moving in relation to the referenced beam of light. For the time being, whenever anyone traveling at a steady speed measures the speed of light in empty space, she always comes up with the same answer: 186,282 miles per second, regardless of how fast or in what direction she may be moving.

This knowledge prompts the questions: "Does God travel

with impunity throughout His creations? "Does He obey the cosmic speed limit?" After all, yesterday, today, and forever are ever before His view in one eternal round, and He is "the Great I AM, Alpha and Omega, the beginning and the end, and the same which looked upon the wide expanse of eternity, and all the seraphic hosts of heaven, before the world was made." (D&C 38:1-2). When the arrow of time flies through eternity, it travels in two directions, both forward and backward at once and forever, without regard to the spatial limitations and temporal constraints of the absolute speed limit of the physical universe that are etched in stone: 186,282 miles per second (299,792,458 meters per second).

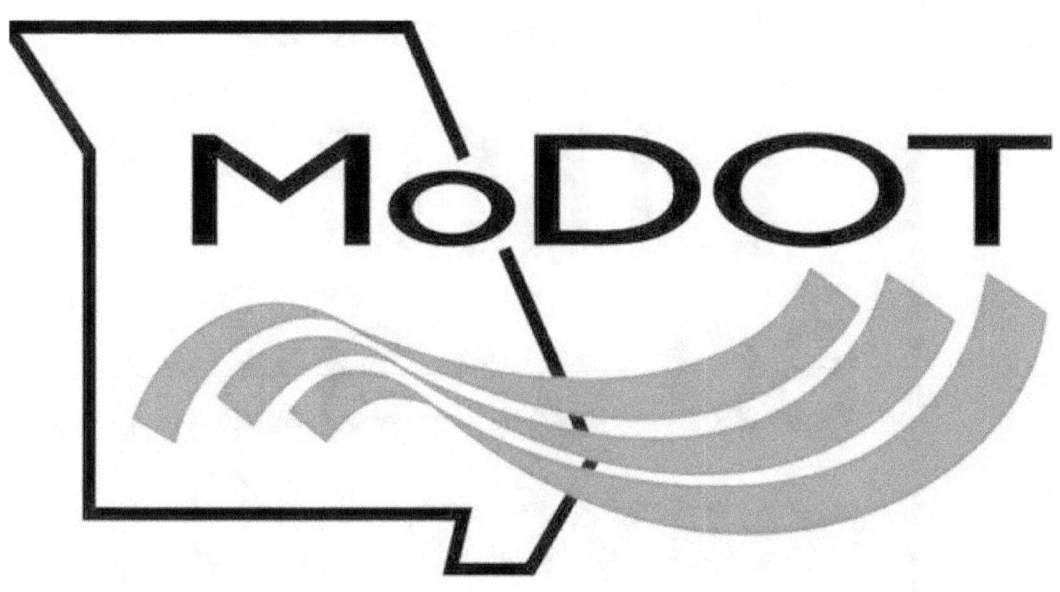

SPEED LIMIT 80 or 85, maybe 90 but don't go 100!

Speed Limit

There must be a
very good reason why God
arranged for us to move along
on the Highways and Byways of Life
at a relative snail's pace. Could it be
that He has blessed us with time, that
we might consider His creations
and witness that He moves
in majesty and power?

On the earth, when we measure a beam of sunlight, its speed is 186,282 miles per second. If we were to fly in a spaceship toward the Sun at half the speed of light and measure the speed of the same beam as it travels earthward, it would be 186,282 miles per second. If we turn the ship around and fly back home at half the speed of light, the same beam of sunlight overtaking us does so at 186,282 miles per second. No matter our speed or direction, that beam of light always travels at exactly the same speed, relative to our velocity.

Gradually, it dawns on us that Gospel principles relating to the eternities just might supersede physical laws relating to the temporal universe. Those who are "born of him" may be oriented more to the expansive laws of the eternal world than to the restrictive laws of the physical world. "Whatsoever is born of God overcometh the world" and is free of the confinements of the equations of mathematics and the limitations of the laws of physics in an inexplicable, indescribable and yet undeniable way. (1 John 5:3).

In the temporal universe, the speed of light is always the same by everyone's measurement, no matter how fast or slow they may be moving in relation to the light that is being measured. Nature accomplishes this trick because the judgments of space and time are "relative" or "private" for each observer. Therefore, if you were on the earth, and another person were on a spacecraft, you would both get the same answer when measuring the speed of the same beam of light. It would be 186,282 miles per second. The simple explanation is that time slows down as we move faster.

The Theory of Relativity tells us that there are no privileged frames of reference. The galaxies are attached to space and imbedded in time, while its fabric is constantly expanding. Interestingly, theories have been postulated that fit the observable universe only back to a point just after its Creation. Physical phenomena have been mathematically mapped out back to a few milliseconds this side of the theoretical Big Bang. At that point, just at the moment of singularity, the laws of physics break down. Under different circumstances that fall outside the parameters of the observable universe, however, other laws with which we are unfamiliar might operate.

Ultimately, if we substitute the term "Creation" for "Big Bang" and ask where and when it took place, the answer is everywhere and forever. No one can say whether God utilized the laws of physics when He formed the worlds, but what we do know is that "by him, were all things created, that are in heaven, and that are in earth, visible and invisible, whether they be thrones, or dominions, or principalities, or powers." (Colossians 1:16). This leaves the door ajar for theologians to testify that God was in control of the creation, and it also allows us to stand back and take a collective deep breath in order to see more clearly that "there is no end to virtue; there is no end to might; there is no end to wisdom, (and) there is no end to light. There is no end to union; there is no end to youth; there is no end to priesthood; (and) there is no end to truth. There is no end to glory; there is no end to love, (and in fact) there is no end to being" itself in the limitless expanse of God's universe where Speed Limits do not apply. (William W. Phelps, "If You Could Hie to Kolob").

Speed Reduced Ahead

Even as we encounter signs along the Highways and Byways of Life that caution us to reduce our speed, the physical constants of our temporal universe demand that we interact with the world around us at one velocity that is nothing short of the speed of light.

We are enveloped in light, in the form of photons, which are the elementary quanta of radiant energy in the universe. Photons not only give us the "colors" of the visible portion of the electromagnetic spectrum, but they also provide the unseen energy that falls in the near, mid, and far infrared portion of the EM spectrum.

Photons expand outward at all times and in all directions and do not require a medium through which to travel. Moving through the vacuum of space, they easily penetrate its immensity. They are immune to external influences, (with the exception of gravity) are found everywhere in the universe, and define its borders even as it infinitely expands (at 186,282 miles per second?) Similarly, the Creator Who is "the Light of the world", also describes

Himself as "Alpha and Omega", and as "the Beginning and the End." He is the eternal "I Am." (He is surely the force behind gravity, which would explain its unusual effect upon light, referenced above).

We use "light" as a metaphor for the presence of the Holy Ghost, in part because it is the most impressive phenomenon in the universe, traveling through its vacuum at a constant velocity of 299,792.458 k.p.s. or 186,282 m.p.s. Nothing can move more quickly than light and still obey the laws of physics, as we understand them. (But, of course, to God, all things are possible. See Matthew 19:26).

It is interesting that the generation of light requires a contribution of energy, whereas there is a negative accounting with darkness. In our temporal world, light (or photons) are produced within atoms when electrons that have been energized to move to higher, less stable, orbits fall back to their natural path around the nucleus. In the process, a photon of energy is given off from the atom in a spontaneous emission of radiation, and if its energy falls within 500 and 800 nanometers in the electromagnetic spectrum, our eyes perceive it as visible light. Photons represent the elemental particles and forces of nature that allow us to visually interact with our environment.

Every photon in the universe (and there are untold numbers of them) is the tangible result of the "Big Bang", the phenomenon that created our physical world in the first place. That event generated heat on an unimaginable scale, around 4 trillion degrees Celsius, when all the matter in the universe was a "quark soup" whose brilliance was incomprehensible.

At that moment of Planck time (the smallest observable unit of time, around 10^{-43} seconds, the time before which the laws of physics fail to describe the universe) light in the form of photonic energy was "everywhere." It filled the rapidly expanding physical universe, which today is a spherical shell approximately 15.9 billion light years from the common center. But at that time, it was a "gravitational singularity", or "spacetime singularity", wherein the quanta normally used to measure our three spatial dimensions and one temporal dimension become infinitely small in a way that does not depend upon any coordinate system. The Law of Conservation of Energy requires that the sum total of the elemental quanta of radiant energy created at the moment of the Big Bang, or light, is still present in our expanding universe. So, if we are tempted to Reduce our Speed as we travel along the Highways and Byways of Life, perhaps we should reconsider. As was aforementioned, we interact with our environment at the speed of light.

Some 13.7 billion years after The Big Bang, heat is still the best way to stimulate the atoms that were then created. Perhaps it is no coincidence that the Holy Ghost can energize us in similar ways. For example, when we consider the value of a suggestion, we "warm up to the idea." Like the cosmic microwave background radiation of 2.725° Kelvin from the Big Bang that lingers everywhere, the light that washes over God's creations, the heat of Light of Christ, and the warm and inviting influence of the Holy Ghost, are just waiting to be detected, absorbed, and applied to practical applications.

The next time you hear someone say: "If you can't stand the heat, get out of the kitchen," consider the cosmic ramifications of the statement. And the next time you see a sign up ahead on the Highways and Byways of Life tempting you to Slow Down, remember that the Lord has given you fire in the bones to prepare you for the day when you, too, will dwell in everlasting burnings.

Speed Up

When we move
from the Highways
and Byways of Life into
eternity, the time constraints
that had been associated with
the cosmic speed limit will lose
all significance, and "See you
later", will cease to be
in our vocabulary.

When time is no longer a part of the equation, the speed limit will effectively be repealed. Time, that we too frequently viewed as a predator that stalked us all our lives, may then only be remembered as a companion that accompanied us on our journey through mortality, reminding us to cherish every moment. In eternity, we will find that the perspective we believed to be unique was faulty, and we will be surprised to learn that mortality was not our natural dimension. We will understand why we were never entirely comfortable upon the Highways and Byways of Life, and why we were "strangers and pilgrims on the earth." (Hebrews 11:13). This, in turn, will explain our innate thrust always toward the future, always beyond the horizon, and always with the pedal to the metal. We will understand more clearly why Captain Jean Luc Picard said that space was the final frontier.

We may even find that growing "old" at the rate of one day every twenty-four hours was strictly and uniquely a quality of mortality and a brilliant mechanism designed by Heavenly Father to afford us an opportunity to gauge the approach of our reunion with Him in the eternal world. We may discover that because we lived in only one dimly lighted corner of reality, it was difficult for us to really appreciate the power of our position and our potential, that we might one day "flourish in immortal youth, unhurt amidst the war of elements, the wreck of matter, and the crash of worlds." (Joseph Addison, "Cato", Act 5, Scene 1).

From our very narrow mortal perspective, frozen in time as it were, we may have grown complacent in our indifference to the subtle messages reflected in its passage. And all the while, we thought that, though we might heed the admonition to go faster, we would forever be constrained by the cosmic speed limit.

Our transition to eternity will thrust upon us the realization that time and space are unnatural dimensions in which we, as eternal beings, cannot be completely comfortable. We will suddenly realize that they are transitory by definition, and it might have only been an illusion that made it seem that it was we who moved through them, when it was really the other way around.

In our youth, time never seemed to pass quickly enough, and we always wanted "our own space." Perhaps we were so recently removed from the eternal world, that we were impatient to return to that more natural environment.

In any event, we might look back and realize that as we approached the terminator line between mortality and immortality, our perception of space and of the passage of time changed again; the former shrank while the latter seemed to speed up.

For now, we occupy three-dimensional space and move in one direction through time at the precise rate of one day in every 23 hours 56 minutes and 4 seconds (a sideral day). We can be certain that the boundaries of the seas, land, sun, moon, and stars will continue to be mathematically defined by physical scientists with greater and greater precision, even as they are esoterically debated by theologians and philosophers alike. But we also have the assurance that the relationship between these boundaries and the metaphysical thrones, dominions, principalities and powers that relate to the heavens will be revealed when the Spirit opens the eyes of our understanding to undreamed of vistas of otherwise inaccessible experience.

For example, how can we now comprehend the scope of Moroni's promise that "by the power of the Holy Ghost (we) may know the truth of all things?" (Moroni 10:5). Certainly, the truth will set us free from the limitations of ignorance so that we may be as one with the majestic clockwork, "like a bird that, pausing in her flight a while on boughs to light, feels them give way beneath her and yet sings, knowing that she hath wings." (Victor Hugo). The expansive depth and breadth of our comprehension will finally put to rest the debates that have preoccupied travelers on the Highways and Byways of Life since the dawn of the Age of Reason.

As we Speed Up, we will soar to new heights as science and religion work in harmony to clarify our understanding of our place in the universe and in the eternities.

Stay Awake

> We cannot afford to allow
> ourselves to be lulled into a false
> sense of security, as we move along the
> Highways and Byways of Life. The nature
> of our long journey can be tedious
> at times, and it can be hypnotic.
> It can dull our senses and
> mesmerize us, until we
> are past feeling.

The Lord, Who created the highways upon which we undertake life's journey, knew beforehand the risks that would be involved in the undertaking. He saw the heart of His people, that it might wax gross, and that their ears might be dull of hearing, and that their eyes might be closed; "lest they should see with their eyes, and hear with their ears, and understand with their heart, and should be converted, and (He) should heal them." (Acts 28:27).

Our travel itinerary, that was created by our Father in Heaven, provided us with the companionship of the Holy Ghost. He would become our greatest countermeasure to boredom or apathy. Our Father gave us the technological wonder of prayer, so that even if we were out of the range of cell service, open lines of communication with Him would always be available, that we might "conquer Satan", who would be abroad in the land", and that we might "escape the hands of (his servants) that do uphold his work." (D&C 10:5).

We have the assurance that God "will not suffer (us) to be so distracted by Satan, or to be so numb to the better angels of our nature, that we would lose our orientation on the Highways and Byways of Life, and be unable to make our way to safe ground. (See 1 Corinthians 10:13).

He will not leave us to fight our battles alone, unless we rashly decline His invitation to awaken our faculties to His assistance from the unseen world. He weighs in on one side of the scale, and the counterfeit coin of Satan's spurious currency clatters down in a cacophony of confusion on the other side of the scale. One vote really does count, and our destiny hangs in the balance.

Ultimately, on every issue there are only three significant votes cast. Our Father votes in favor of us, and Satan votes against us. We cast the deciding vote as all eternity holds its collective breath and waits in hushed anticipation to see what the outcome will be. At that instant, there is no yesterday, and there is no tomorrow. There is only this moment in time, when we are truly awake to possibilities that we may have never before considered, when we have the privilege to determine whether or not we will govern our lives by listening to the voice of the Spirit.

If we choose wisely, we will shake off our drowsiness and find ourselves on the path to glory. We will no longer be lulled to sleep by beguiling lullabies, but will be awakened and alive to divine possibilities, as the Highways and Byways of Life lead us to the gates of the Celestial Kingdom.

Stay In Your Lane

When we are evenly yoked to the Savior and have the discipline of faith, we Stay in Our Lane. We have no reason to deviate in our obedience.

Our faith is like a screw that is slowly twisted in to a solid piece of wood. With each turn, the anchor becomes more sure. Ultimately, it is solid. The screw cannot be removed unless fear loosens the screw, turn by turn, inexorably weakening our hold on the truth that we want to secure with the discipline of faith.

The anchor of our faith is sure as long as the screw remains in place. What is fascinating, though, is that the energy that had been expended to turn in the screw will have done its job, leaving us free to direct our attention elsewhere. But the result of the expenditure of faith will remain steadfast.

This repetitive process allows us to expand the scope of our faith to infinite proportion, until every particle of our faith has been stabilized. It helps us to understand the teachings of Joseph Smith, that "faith is not only the principle of action, but of power also, in all intelligent beings, whether in heaven or on earth. ("Lectures on Faith", 1:13-14). "The principle of power which existed in the bosom of God, by which the worlds were framed, was faith; and it is by reason of this principle of power existing in the Deity, that all created things exist; so that all things in heaven, on earth, or under the earth exist by reason of faith as it existed in Him. Had it not been for the principle of faith the worlds would never have been framed neither would man have been formed of the dust. It is the principle by which Jehovah works, and through which he exercises power over all temporal as well as eternal things. Take this principle or attribute ... from the Deity, and he would cease to exist. (" Lectures on Faith", 1:13-16).

"Faith, then, is the first great governing principle which has power, dominion, and authority over all things; by it they exist, by it they are upheld, by it they are changed, and by it they remain, agreeable to the will of God. Without it there is no power, and without power there could be no creation nor existence!" ("Lectures on Faith", 1:24).

"We here observe that God is the only supreme governor and independent being in whom all fullness and perfection dwell; who is omnipotent, omnipresent and omniscient; without beginning of days or end of life; and that in him every good gift and every good principle dwell; and that he is the Father of lights; in him the principle of faith dwells independently." ("Lectures on Faith", 2:2)

New Hampshire DOT
Department of Transportation

Steep Grade Ahead

The path
that lies before
us may seem too
steep, or too twisty,
or too hazardous to
even make the attempt.
At moments like this, we
just need to trust the Lord
Who sees the end from the
beginning. He has traveled
the road before us and
He knows what our
capabilities are,
and He is our
guide.

Wrote the poet: "My life is but a weaving between my Lord and me; I cannot choose the colors. He worketh steadily. Oft times He weaveth sorrow, and I, in foolish pride, forget He sees the upper, and I the under side. Not 'til the loom is silent, and the shuttles cease to fly, shall God unroll the canvas, and explain the reason why. The dark threads are as needful in the Weaver's skillful hand, as the threads of gold and silver in the pattern He has planned." (Benjamin Malachi Franklin).

"Everyone must climb the Hill of Difficulty alone, and

since there is no royal road to the summit, I must zigzag it in my own way. I slip back many times; I fall; I stand still; I run against the edge of hidden obstacles; I lose my temper and find it again and keep it better. I trudge on; I gain a little; I feel encouraged; I get more eager and climb higher and begin to see the widening horizon. Every struggle is a victory. One more effort and I reach the luminous cloud, the blue depths of the sky, the uplands of my desire." (Helen Keller, "The Story of My Life").

Stop Ahead

In a sense,
the Gospel exists
to help us to return
to the secret garden
of our childhood that
was conceived as the
best place for us to
fully mature to the
full stature of
our spirits.

As William Henry Wordsworth wrote: "Heaven lies about us in our infancy. Shades of the prison house begin to close upon the growing boy, but he beholds the light and whence it flows. He sees it in his joy. The youth, who daily farther from the east must travel, still is nature's priest, and by the vision splendid, is on his way attended. At length the man perceives it die away, and fade into the light of common day." ("Ode: Intimations of Immortality").

Fortunately, a "Haz-Mat Protocol" has been written into The Plan that "de-toxifies" us from the cares and conditioning influences of the world and from the homogenization process that occurs as adults are worn down by the vicissitudes of life. It allows us to be born again, to become as little children at play, and to be repetitively re-vitalized, as we are re-introduced, along the Highways and Byways of Life, to that Magical Kingdom where dreams really do come true.

Stop Complaining

Those who are
chronic complainers
habitually speak out of
both sides of their mouths at
the same time, suffering, in the
process, from a confusion of
languages. Their distorted
words reflect a vacuum
of values, a paucity
of principles, and
a divine-center
deficiency.

Complaint often consists of vague and inconsistent language that builds on the shifting sands of moral relativism, situational ethics, and secular humanism. These are the favorite playgrounds of those with golden tongues.

It is far too easy to quiet our consciences with the soothing and false counsel of "foolish and blind guides", illogical though they may be. (Helaman 13:29). In all too many ways, when we ignorantly enlist in the army of chronic complainers, we are substituting sophistry for the Almighty. No matter that complaint is often a deception and an illusion, that panders to an audience that is only too eager to trade celestial sureties for telestial trinkets and to sell its divine birthright for a mess of pottage.

Some on Life's Highways and Byways are content only as long as their travels take them to well-traveled avenues dotted with conveniently located rest stops, and to brightly lighted world stages filled with the appreciative applause and laudatory comments of fawning followers. But placed in challenging settings with no-one looking, when there have been no preparatory fortifying experiences, and when there is no positive peer pressure to sustain correct choices, it is far easier to find fault.

How much better to determine to express ourselves with words that are tools and not weapons. We ponder and pray, rather than wander and play. We avoid assumptions, speculation, and second-guessing. We plumb the depths of issues, rather than skim the shallows of idle chatter. We prefer substance to superficiality. We are good listeners, and when we do speak, it is with purpose. We value trust in relationships, and then act with confidence and in good faith. Sometimes, even the best of us need to bite our tongues, as we retrench and tap in to the power of positive thinking.

STOP
DISTRACTED DRIVING

Stop Distracted Driving

From out
of heaven we hear
the angels crying Oyez,
Oyez Oyez! We honor our
Father in Heaven when we
give Him our patient
and undivided
attention.

If we cease to engage in Distracted Driving while navigating the Highways and Byways of Life, the Holy Ghost will give us enough light to take a few steps into the unknown. (See D&C 84:46). God will endow our spiritual heartstrings with the ability to resonate with recognition when we encounter truth. We will "discard the poor lenses of the body, and peer through the telescope of truth into the infinite reaches of immortality." (Helen Keller, "My Religion", p. 76).

When we Stop Distracted Driving, we will be able to block out the trivial, and only hear God's entreaties in the purest form of concentration. Input from the five natural senses will be transformed by the spiritual sixth sense. We will be conditioned through diligence, discipline, faith, and patience, to move beyond our physical resources to address the concerns of greatest importance.

But of those who are preoccupied with telestial trivia, and who casually and superficially receive the enlightenment that would have been so freely given, the Lord has warned: "Wo unto him ... that wasteth the days of his probation, for awful is his state!" (2 Nephi 9:27). Those who are Distracted while Driving upon the Highways and Byways of Life may be more susceptible to groan under darkness, as they grope about in a frantic and yet fruitless search for meaning and stability in text messaging and Snap Chat. (See D&C 84:49).

If we ignore our innate urge to be drawn to the Light, and instead allow ourselves to be habitually distracted by trivial concerns, we risk settling for a life in a "second-class hotel" of our own making. There is, after all, "a tide in the affairs of men, which, taken at the flood, leads on to fortune. Omitted, all the voyage of their life is bound in shallows and in miseries." (Shakespeare, Brutus, in "Julius Caesar", Act 4, Scene 2).

Anything that shuts out all the wonderful things of which our minds and spirits are capable, leaving them drugged in a state of thoughtless stupor, is sin. For the same reasons, Joseph Smith wrote from Liberty Jail "how vain and trifling have been our conferences, our councils, our meetings, our private as well as public conversations. Too low, too mean, too vulgar, too condescending for the dignified characters called and chosen of God." (Quoted by Lucy Mack Smith, "History of Joseph Smith", p. 55).

When Captain Moroni addressed what he perceived to be the great neglect of the government officials of his day, he asked: "Can you think to sit upon your thrones in a state of thoughtless stupor?" (Alma 60:6-7). Moroni believed that these bureaucrats had lost their bearings on eternity. Had they been Distracted while Driving along the Highways and Byways of Life, the temporal and spiritual welfare of the citizens of their society would have hung in the balance. Heaven always holds its breath while waiting upon our initiative to be guided by the Spirit.

Another symptom of Distracted Driving is the loss of our spiritual equilibrium. To bring it back into be a supposed state of balance, we often adjust our values as a quick fix. We worship gods of wood and stone and justify it as multiculturalism. We embrace perversion and legitimize it as an alternative lifestyle. Transgression is redefined as misbehavior, and sin is repackaged as poor judgment. Robbery becomes undocumented shopping. We exploit the poor in the name of government-sponsored lotteries with the promise that anyone can become a millionaire. When unborn children are killed, the collective conscience is soothed by calling it pro-choice. Power is abused in the name of progressivism. When the media is polluted with obscenities, it is characterized as freedom of expression. When we are caught in a lie, we rationalize it as hyper-exaggeration. The target is moved so many times that those who are thus distracted think they are scoring repetitive bulls-eyes, when in reality the arrows have strayed far from the mark.

In all of the above scenarios, it is better to run our wipers a few times to remove the bugs from our windshield, switch on our headlights, turn off all media, place both hands of the wheel, and keep our eyes fixed on the road, in order to Avoid Distracted Driving on the Highways and Byways of Life.

STOP DROWSY DRIVING

Stop Drowsy Driving

At times,
we all need to
step back and take
a deep cleansing breath,
so that we may then sharpen
our saw. Having said that, after
a refreshing pause, we need to be
able to recognize when "it is high
time to awake out of sleep: for
now is our salvation nearer
than when we believed."
(Romans 13:11).

When our senses are dulled and our priorities are out of order, however, we lose power. If we choose mediocrity, rationalization, selfish pleasure, things of the world, the honors of men, or disobedience, we lose power. As long as we remain lethargic, we will never partake of the fruit of the tree of life, enjoy its delicious fruit, or feel real gratitude. After taking a deep cleansing breath, we should seek to obtain the word of truth, for then our tongue will be loosed, and we will have the Spirit and "the power of God unto the convincing of men." (D&C 11:21).

Stop Gossiping

Words that are
carelessly scattered
about by the wind on the
Highways and Byways of
Life suggest that we
have brought our
mouths online
before our
brains.

Gossiping is a kindred spirit of murmuring, but it is more focused on mindless chatter and speaking without real purpose. It is just as damaging, however, because it feeds voraciously on rumor, second-hand information, innuendo, and vanity. Left unchecked, it may build into a self-perpetuating chain reaction leading to a cascade of unfortunate consequences. Its many forms have one common characteristic. The words so loosely spoken cannot be gathered up later on. Like feathers left on the doorstep of those with whom one engages in idle conversation, they will have drifted to the four winds, and they cannot be recalled.

Stop Grumbling

Grumbling, is the
subdued and continually repeated
expression of indistinct or inarticulate
complaint. Grumbling can build like an
earthquake into harmonic waves with the
power to undermine the foundations of
relationships and institutions, which
are the features upon which the
Highways and Byways of
Life are built.

Those who grumble expect results without responsibility; thus, it is a cowardly act. While it is often conducted anonymously or in the cloak of secrecy, its effect is felt publicly. Those who grumble want a tangible return without having made a legitimate initial investment.

Perhaps those who grumble do so because they are as "children, tossed to and fro, and carried about with every wind of doctrine, by the sleight of men, and cunning craftiness." (Ephesians 4:14). Those who stand for nothing will typically fall for anything; they curse the darkness, without ever thinking to light a candle. They lack a strong will, but make up for it with an even stronger won't. They do not understand that "fame is a vapor, and popularity is an accident, and those who cheer you today may curse you tomorrow. In the end, the only thing that endures is character." (Anonymous)

Those who grumble, and murmur against the Church, often have only a weak foundation of doctrinal understanding of the Gospel, and risk falling into transgression in consequence of their shallow comprehension of principles. Picking apart the scriptures can distort the doctrines into meaningless fragments without any coherent connection. As Alma declared to the inhabitants of Ammonihah, "Behold, the scriptures are before you; if ye will wrest them, it shall be to your own destruction." (Alma 13:20).

Grumbling can distract us from completing the labor to which we have been called. Until our actions reflect our commitment, we cannot make sustained progress.

Stop, Look, and Listen

At times, along the Highways and Byways of Life, we get caught up in its hectic pace. We need to be reminded to be still, in order to know that God is there. (See Psalms 46:10). We need to Stop, Look, and Listen.

When the angel of the Lord descended from heaven after the death and resurrection of the Savior, "his countenance was like lightning, and his raiment white as snow." (Matthew 28:2-3). As the Psalmist recorded: "His lightnings enlightened the world, (and) the earth saw, and trembled." (Psalms 97:4). Perhaps "thunderings and lightnings" are the best way to describe how conversation between the Gods in the Celestial Kingdom would sound to mortal ears. (Revelation 8:5). God's testimony, after all, is "the voice of thunderings, and the voice of lightnings." (D&C 88:90).

"And the temple of God was opened in heaven, and there was seen in his temple the ark of his testament: and there were lightnings, and voices, and thunderings." (Revelation 11:19). "And it came to pass" that there was "a thick cloud upon the mount, and the voice of the trumpet exceeding loud, so that all the people that (were) in the camp (of

Israel) trembled." (Exodus 19:16). Everyone in that company shared a common experience, as their raw nerve endings were touched by the power and influence of God. "And all the people saw the thunderings, and the lightnings, and the noise of the trumpet, and the mountain smoking." (Exodus 20:18).

"And out of the throne (of God) proceeded lightnings and thunderings and voices." (Revelation 4:5). "When he uttereth his voice, there is a multitude of waters in the heavens, and he causeth the vapours to ascend from the ends of the earth. He maketh lightnings with rain, and bringeth forth the wind." (Jeremiah 10:13). "How oft have I called", He asked, "by the voice of thunderings, and by the voice of lightnings, (D&C 43:25). "And the voice of his word", wrote Daniel, "was like the voice of a multitude. (Daniel 10:6).

At the end of the day, as Rabindranath Tagore mused, there will be eye-kissing and heart-sweetening light that dances at the center of our lives and strikes the chords of our love. And there will be butterflies that spread their sails on a sea of light, with lilies and jasmine that surge up on the wave crests of light that is shattered into gold on every cloud and scattered in profusion as gemstones. This is the familiar light that is the province of all those who have been born again into a newness of life.

This is the light that reminds us to Stop, Look, and Listen, as we travel the Highways and Byways of Life; to remember that on one special evening two thousand years ago, there was no darkness at all, "but it was as light as though it was midday. And it came to pass that the sun did rise in the morning again, according to its proper order. And they knew that it was the day that the Lord should be born." (3 Nephi 1:19).

In the scriptures, the first recorded words of Heavenly Father were: "Let there be light." (Genesis 1:3). His last recorded words were "This is my beloved Son, Hear Him." (J.S.H. 1:17). These two verses are inextricably linked and are book ends to our faith. Our own sun rises and falls on our desire to be dazzled by His light and to be mesmerized by His magic. (But only if we Stop, Look, and Listen).

During the course of our lives, there are probably many questions we will never be able to answer. The reassurance, "In time, you will understand." may not be entirely valid, for mortality impels us to see through a glass darkly. At some point, when time no longer exists, we will be able to "go forth from our dwelling place and discarding the poor lenses of the body, peer through the telescope of truth into the infinite reaches of immortality." (Helen Keller).

Take Responsibility

*On the Highways
and Byways of Life,
if we plan our work and
then work our plan, if we
Take Responsibility for the
process as well as for the
outcomes, we will reach
our destination.*

We know that proper prior planning prevents poor priesthood performance. We dream big, but by establishing deadlines to fulfil our dreams, we create realistic goals. We know by our own experience that work without vision is drudgery, and that vision without work is dreamery, but that work with vision is destiny. It is because we Take Responsibility that we know these things.

We know that there is a God in heaven, because we witness all around us, on the Highways and Byways of Life, the universality of responsibility, that is a quality with which God has blessed both man and beasts. High levels of responsibility are found within those who are disciples of Christ, but they do not enjoy exclusive access to its energizing influence. Responsibility is not found solely within the human family, but is common among those with whom we share the rungs on the evolutionary ladder. Anyone who has gotten between an agitated cow moose and her calf or has seen a momma bear aggressively protecting her cubs has witnessed primal manifestations of responsibility. It drives the behavior of countless other species, but it runs deeply in our own blood, as well.

John K. Edmunds enjoyed a long and distinguished legal career in Chicago. One day, a widow came to him for advice, and when they were finished, she apprehensively asked: "How much do I owe you?" Gently, he responded, "Why don't you pay me what you think it's worth. Greatly relieved, she got out her coin purse, fished around for a quarter, and pressed it into his hand. He looked at the quarter, looked at her, and then got out his own coin purse, and gave her ten cents change.

Howard W. Hunter must have been referring to this level of responsibility, when he counseled: "We need to walk more resolutely and more charitably the path that Jesus has shown. We need to pause to help and lift another, and surely we will find strength beyond our own. If we would do more to learn the healer's art, there would be untold chances to use it, to touch the wounded and the weary, and to show to all a gentle heart."

Responsibility begins with a strong sense of intention or focus, but that is only half of the preliminary equation. The second half defines a statement of purpose or a plan of action. The difficulty is that we make promises about behaviors and outcomes with our sense of intention or focus, but we ignore the process necessary to achieve the goal. Envisioned outcomes should be the end-product of that dynamic flow of process. If we learn to commit fully to the process, then the outcomes will be what they should be.

But, if we commit merely to the outcomes and ignore the process, we sabotage both. The unequal demands of intention on the one hand, and our lack of purpose or a plan of action on the other, will condemn any hope of success. Day in and day out, that success is largely determined by our capacity to act with responsibility. Each time we stoop down to lift a wounded soul, we keep a date with destiny, and reach greater heights of achievement.

The follow-through element of responsibility is that God "worketh in (us) both to will and to do of his good pleasure." (Philippians 2:13, underlining mine). Once we have established a habit pattern of responsibility, we follow the admonition of Paul, to "perform the doing of it; that as there was a readiness to will, so there may be a performance also out of that which (we) have." (2 Corinthians 8:11, underlining mine).

The Gospel has taught us how to recognize the process that is necessary to follow in order to achieve envisioned outcomes. We know that we must act with responsibility; "whole-souled, deeply held, eternally cherished commitment to the principles we know to be true." (Howard W. Hunter). We have learned to make the distinction between the responsibility of total commitment and a insipid contribution to the cause. We remember the story of the chicken and a pig who were invited to a breakfast, and how the chicken said that he would bring some eggs. He asked the pig if he would provide bacon, to which the pig replied: Yours is a contribution, but mine is a sacrifice. Latter-day Saints know that, ultimately, "what our Father in Heaven will require of us is more than a contribution; it is a total commitment, a complete devotion; all that we are and all that we can be." (Howard W. Hunter).

If we consider our commitment to act with responsibility, we might ask ourselves: If the Lord put His finger to our pulse, would He be able to detect the quickening influence of the Spirit? If He measured our core testimony temperature, would it reflect a burning zeal to embrace the principles of the Gospel? Would our actions betray our desire to do everything we could do to come unto Christ? Would we love God and our neighbors as ourselves? Would our actions reflect who we are and what we believe? If we were on trial, would there be enough evidence to convict us of being Christians?

Are we pressing forward with complete dedication and steadfastness, with confidence and a firm determination in Christ, having a perfect brightness of hope and perfect faith; with charity, or a love of God and of all men? Are we feasting upon the word of Christ, receiving strength and nourishment from the scriptures?

Do we listen to the Spirit and constantly seek its direction? Do we pray for the strength to meet our challenges? Do we set our hearts upon the riches of eternity, rather than the things of the world? Do we recognize that spiritual renewal will always trump physical gratification? Have we made a choice regarding whom we will serve? Do we strengthen our brethren? Are we anxious to share our joy? Do we put into action our beliefs? Are we anxiously engaged in bringing to pass many good things of our own free will? Do we love one another? Do we keep ourselves unspotted from the world? Do we stand firm, and are we true and living members of the Church? Does our level of responsibility betray the reality that we have received the promise to be among those "who are come unto Mount Zion, and unto the city of the living God, the heavenly place, the holiest of all?" (D&C 76:66).

Thank You
FOR SLOWING DOWN

214

Thank You For Slowing Down

When Heavenly Father created The
Highways and Byways of Life, He did
so with the anticipation that we
would take time to pause
and reflect upon our
good fortune.

Paul wrote to the Thessalonian Saints that they should "pray without ceasing." (1 Thessalonians 5:17). Amulek enlarged upon this principle, and counseled the Zoramites: "After ye have done these things, if ye turn away the needy, and the naked, and visit not the sick and afflicted, and impart of your substance, if ye have, to those who stand in need, behold your prayer is vain and availeth you nothing, and ye are as hypocrites who do deny the faith." (Alma 34:28). The Savior warned against meaningless prayer, however, devoid of substance, and helped His disciples to understand how to avoid such a practice. "When ye pray", he cautioned, "use not vain repetitions, as the heathen do: for they think that they shall be heard for their much speaking." (Matthew 6:7). Prayer is "in vain" when it is reduced to the status of an academic exercise, when it is an empty and meaningless ritual, performed by rote, without effect, or without the desired or intended result. To "try in vain" is to try without success, but it is more (or less) than that. It is to try half-heartedly. Meaningless prayer is blasphemous because it uses the Lord's name improperly and without authority. Those who do so are imposters, invoking the name of Deity in a false, misleading, and counterfeit way. We blaspheme the name of God when we invoke His Holy name unsuccessfully because of our unworthiness, or when we invoke His name without purpose, or without expectation of meaningful dialogue with the heavens.

We guard against falling into hypocrisy and denying the faith, or against praying in vain, when we ratchet down the pace of our lives, and stop to smell the roses, or take off our shoes in the presence of God, as the case may be. For "earth is crammed with heaven, and every common bush with fire of God. But only those who see, take off their shoes. The rest stand around picking blackberries." (Elizabeth Barrett Browning, "Aurora Leigh," book 7, lines 822-823).

The Future: Just Ahead

1,449 verses
in the Book of Mormon
state a life-preserving truth:
"It came to pass." It did not
come to stay! Life unfolds
before our eyes, often
in surprisingly
delightful
ways.

Dreamers on the Highways and Byways of Life imagine things that never were, and ask "Why not?" They work through their problems, instead of working around them. They find mentors to emulate, instead of scapegoats to blame. They look for better solutions, instead of easier ways. When they make mistakes, they readily acknowledge them, instead of shifting the blame. In pressure situations, they remember previous victories, instead of past defeats. They keep their faces oriented toward the light, so the shadows will always be behind them. They realize that they cannot go back and start a new beginning, but they can rely upon the Atonement of Jesus Christ to write a new ending. They have confidence in His ability to create self-fulfilling prophecies. They believe in His divine design, and that their lives are "fairy tales waiting to be written by His hand." (Hans Christian Anderson).

Think Before You Speak

There is always the possibility that, notwithstanding our previous service or righteousness, we "may fall from grace" or from good standing in the sight of Deity, "and depart from the living God" (D&C 20:32). Thus, as we move along Life's Highways and Byways, we need to always consider what we are about to do before we speak, for "as a man thinketh in his heart, so is he." (Proverbs 23:7).

In our day, Babylon has become firmly entrenched in the world, and the cesspool of her polluting influence even encroaches upon the foundations of the Church and Kingdom, and threatens to corrupt, compromise, or undermine them. She is "the great whore that sitteth upon many waters, with whom the kings of the earth have committed fornication." (Revelation 17:1-2). To some extent, all who have entered into a wicked and idolatrous relationship with the world have been intimate with the whore.

Two of the terrible consequences of the world's fascination with Babylon are spiritual insensitivity and inconsistency, the inevitable results of a withdrawal of the Spirit. Isaiah foresaw such a condition in the Last Days when he wrote: "Stay yourselves, and wonder. cry ye out, and cry: they are drunken, but not with wine. They stagger, but not with strong drink. For the Lord hath poured out upon you the spirit of deep sleep, and hath closed your eyes: the prophets, and your rulers, and seers hath he covered." (Isaiah 29:9-11).

In contrast, the ideal that is expressed in the 9th Article of Faith is repeated for emphasis in the action verb "to believe". "We believe all that God has revealed, all that He does now reveal, and we believe that He will yet reveal many great and important things pertaining to the Kingdom of God."

If we would Think Before We Speak, we need to fine tune our listening ear, for there is no revelation where there is no student. Many people in the world, and even in the Church, deny themselves the blessings of heaven simply because they do not ask for them. The Savior explained how anxious God is to grant the righteous requests of His children. Comparing His benevolence to that of our earthly fathers, His Son declared: "How much more shall your Father who is in heaven give good things to them that ask him?" (3 Nephi 14:11).

We need to Think Before We Speak; to "take heed and pray always, lest (we) fall into temptation." (D&C 20:33). Prayer is a way to exercise faith and is a powerful weapon that can be used to resist the enticements of the devil. We cannot retain the Spirit of the Lord unless we pray.

The Lord is mindful of His covenant relationship with us, and so He requires extraordinary performance of those "who profess (His) name." (D&C 50:4). As professors, we represent ourselves as independent witnesses. We back up our thoughts and words with deeds, as we give vitality, or life, to desire. Our good intentions, after all, are only dreams. Harold B. Lee was fond of reciting the familiar aphorism: "Vision without work is dreamery, and work without vision is drudgery. But work with vision is destiny!"

As professors, we work in partnership with the Holy Ghost to move ever closer to our divine destiny. We are persevering and stay focused on the tasks at hand. We begin with the end in mind and settle for more, and not for less. We are determined, disciplined, focused, and purposeful, and are not easily distracted or persuaded. Our foundation is on bedrock. We have depth and breadth and have made regular deposits to our spiritual bank accounts, from which we may take timely, strategic, and significant withdrawals. We are guided by the Spirit and teach by example. We are leaders, and not just managers. We help others to clarify their own feelings, and the principles we teach are founded on doctrines rather than on values. As professors, we are not easily swayed by conventional wisdom or politically correct ideology and we are uninfluenced by situational ethics or expediency. Aided by the Holy Ghost, we Think Before We Speak.

Thru Traffic: Merge Right

Sometimes,
on the Highways and
Byways of Life, the supposed
detours that lie in our path may
in reality define the shortest
route to our destination.
Perceived obstacles
may facilitate
the flow of
traffic.

Those who have read the dialogue between Edmund Dantès and the priest Abbé Faria that occurred deep within the walls of the prison of the Chateau d'If, in Alexandere Dumas' novel "The Count of Monte Cristo" will understand God's gentle correction in our lives.

"What are you thinking?" asked the Abbé smilingly, imputing the deep abstraction in which his visitor was plunged to the excess of his awe and wonder. "I was reflecting, in the first place", replied Dantès, "upon the enormous degree of intelligence and ability you must have employed to reach the high perfection to which you have attained. What would you not have accomplished if you had been free?"

"Possibly nothing at all", replied the priest. "The overflow of my brain would probably, in a state of freedom, have evaporated in a thousand follies. Misfortune is needed to bring to light the treasures of the human intellect. Compression is needed to explode gunpowder. Captivity has brought my mental faculties to a focus, and you are well aware that from the collision of clouds electricity is produced, and from electricity, lightning, and from lightning, illumination."

Finally, at the end of the tale, Dantès observes: "Only a man who has felt ultimate despair is capable of feeling ultimate bliss. It is necessary to have wished for death, in order to know how good it is to live. Live, then, and be happy, and never forget that, until the day God deigns to reveal the future to us, the sum of human wisdom will be contained in these words: wait and hope."

TOUGH DECISIONS AHEAD

Tough Decisions Ahead

Our Father in Heaven
knew beforehand that there
would be Tough Decisions to be
made by His children, as they
negotiate the Highways
and Byways of Life.

It is for our convenience that He blessed us with the easily recognizable, manageable, and savory reduction sauce of time. We have no other frame of reference, but perhaps mortality is more manageable when we live out or lives in a linear temporal dimension from which there seems to be only one exit somewhere in our future. Our liberation from the inexorable arrow of time will come when we lay aside our mortal clay, clothed in the garments of immortality and eternal life. It is only in that state of existence that we will finally and fully comprehend His work and glory.

In the "meantime", we have the Light of Christ and the gift of the Holy Ghost to prepare us for that inevitable epiphany. (See Moses 1:39). God's stroke of genius in harnessing the quixotic element of time, by apportioning it in discrete increments of seconds, minutes, hours, and so on, allows thought, feeling, and spontaneity to germinate, and to be catalyzed by agency. It gives us pause, that we might have enough "time" to make the Tough Decisions that lie Ahead.

The scriptures record that before the dawn of creation: "The Lord said: Let us go down. And they went down at the beginning, and they, that is the Gods, organized and formed the heavens and the earth." (Abraham 4:1). From an eternal vantage point, the celestial clock was reset. It was calibrated "at the beginning" to a temporal scale by omniscient, omnipotent, and omnipresent Beings, whereas the reckoning had been beforehand "the Lord's time, according to the reckoning of Kolob." (Abraham 3:4).

In a metaphysical process that is far beyond our comprehension, the earth literally fell from Kolob into time as we know it. Its arrow, that had heretofore traveled in all directions simultaneously, was now locked onto just one forward track. At that pivotal moment, a "majestic clockwork" was introduced that set in motion an evolution in thought relating to time, that culminated in Newton's "Principia", and Einstein's Theories of Relativity, ideas that have shaken the foundations of our understanding of physics, or broadly speaking, have mathematically wrestled with the concept of time in an attempt to quantify the natural world. In a process that continues to this day, time was launched into the future like an arrow shot from the bow of God, to point us in the direction of the Tough Decisions that lie Ahead.

In 1916, Einstein unlocked the mercurial side of the nature of time. In a sense, he let the genie out of the bottle. He opened Pandora's Box and unleashed a new definition of time into a world that has struggled ever since to understand its metaphysical implications.

Common folk like us, who are now comfortable with the phrase "It's all relative", seldom recognize the intimate association that expression shares with our exercise of free will and with our comprehension of God. The truth is, that our greater appreciation of the relationships between time and space has come with a sense of relief that, in order to honor the principle of agency, God does not have to cease to be, nor is He required to relinquish His omniscience and omnipotence.

We have the power to do wonderful things with the gifts of time, space, and free will, as we grapple with the Tough Decision that lie Ahead, while simultaneously keeping Heavenly Father firmly in the driver's seat. He remains in control even as power remains in His children, "wherein they are agents unto themselves." (D&C 58:28).

We use special terminology to describe just how empowering the gifts of time and agency can be. Action verbs describe things that we "do", and they presuppose motion in multiple dimensions across a temporal spectrum. We press forward with steadfastness, we feast upon the words of eternal life, we read, we fear, we ponder and pray, we lift the latch, and we force the way. We are bathed in vitality, and we are empowered with an otherworldly serenity.

Our normal lifespan gives us ample opportunity to develop patience as we bide our time, in anticipation of the Tough Decisions that lie Ahead. It allows us to mature in discipline as we take time, to expand our care and concern as we find time, to enhance our thoughtfulness as we spend time, to cultivate wisdom as we invest time, to experience pleasure as we share time, and even to delight in diligence as we make time. Time becomes our steady, measured schoolmaster, and we use it wisely when we engage the curriculum of Christ, as we learn how to make tough decisions along the Highways and Byways of Life. (See Galatians 3:24).

Under normal circumstances, heaven can wait, in order to allow us to enjoy the gift of time and to use it with responsibility. In the motion picture, "Indiana Jones and The Last Crusade", the Grail Knight told Indie: "You must choose. But choose wisely, for as the true Grail will bring you life, the false Grail will take it from you."

The Gospel Plan teaches us how to choose wisely, because it clearly identifies the Holy Grail that must be our quest. Spencer W. Kimball urged: "Do it! Do it right! Do it right now!" because "there's no time like the present; no present like time, and life can be over in the space of a rhyme." (Georgia Byng).

Even the rabbit in Alice's "Wonderland" recognized the value of time well-spent, that had been expended in good decision-making, when he exclaimed to no one in particular: "I'm late! I'm late! For a very important date! No time to say 'Hello!' 'Good-bye!' I'm late, I'm late, I'm late!"

TOW-AWAY ZONE

Tow-Away Zone

The fact that Tow-Away Zones exist along the Highways and Byways of Life suggests that there may be sections of the roadway where the rules of the road no longer exist, and the only options are to boot illegally parked or abandoned vehicles, or tow them to the impound yard.

The corruption of the road may be such that there is no longer a coherent, organized system of signs to govern the flow of traffic.

If we accept the doctrine that there has been an abandonment of signs (some characterize it as an "Apostasy"), namely traffic signs, regulatory signs, warning signs, construction and maintenance signs, service signs, and guidance signs, we then might ask: "What were its causes? Did it take God, who is the Master Planner and Chief Highway Engineer, by surprise? How would such an "apostasy" fit into the overall scope of His divine design? Does The Plan make allowances for those who have had to deal with a dearth of directions? Are there eternally negative consequences as a result of the lack of guidance? Have travelers upon the Highways and Byways of Life been influenced by a long night of darkness?"

Thankfully, today we are in the midst of the restoration of highway signs as they were originally constructed and placed, but at the same time we are assaulted on every front by those who do not believe there is a need for such a drastic remedy. Many feel that it is their self-anointed mission to tear down the new signs that are popping up everywhere. They propose, instead, that we take every spur on the road, or explore every rabbit hole alongside the straight and narrow path, to see if we might discover a variation on The Plan of God that is more suitable to our needs – read "contemporary." But it we get our ticket punched, as it were, by every uninformed skeptic who seems to have a personal agenda to promote, we risk alienating ourselves from God and weakening our faith in foundation principles.

Those who question the testimony of Joseph Smith, or of Andrew Hudson, or of Parker Edwards, are still living in the Great Apostasy. For them, it has not yet ended. Learning can be a dangerous thing if it is not accompanied by the Spirit of God. "O that cunning plan of the evil one! O the vainness, and the frailties, and the foolishness of men! When they are learned they think they are wise, and they hearken not unto the counsel of God, for they set it aside, supposing they know of themselves, wherefore, their wisdom is foolishness and it profiteth them not." (2 Nephi 9:29). Faith is the spiritual strong searchlight that allows all of us to fearlessly take a few steps into the darkness. Only then will He illuminate the way and banish the Tow Away Zones of the Apostasy from our minds and our hearts.

Traction Tires Required

Each of us
desperately needs the
reassurance that the grip
of correct principles provides,
not to mention the guarantee of
the sure-footed stability of doctrine,
as we trace our way past the slippery
slopes that lie above personality
precipices along the Highways
and Byways of Life.

We learn the art of defensive winter driving, as we zip down life's highways and byways, for we know that the fiery darts of the adversary will streak across dark and threatening skies that lie ahead. We become immersed in the construction of an all-terrain vehicle that will provide a fortress of security to guard against the day when the adversary's assaults will surely come. With our memory of the ideological War in Heaven still fresh in our minds, we renew our resolve to keep both hands on the wheel with our minds clear and focused as we valiantly and pointedly promote the cause of Zion with the assurance that comes from increased traction on Gospel sod.

Traffic Fines Doubled in Work Zones

If we are
to be counted
among the Saints in
the household of faith,
we must obey the greatest
of all the commandments.
These are to love God,
and our neighbors
as ourselves.

"Unto whomsoever much is given, of him shall be much required." (Luke 12:48). It may not be stretching it a bit to say that Fines will be Doubled in Work Zones, but it is true that those who sin "against the greater light shall receive the greater condemnation." (D&C 82:3). This underscores the necessity of making sure that we do the right things for the right reasons. We are standing on safe ground, on Gospel sod, when love of God and of our fellow travelers on the Highways and Byways of Life is our motivation for laboring in its Work Zones.

When we are in the service of others, if our efforts are without love, they are insincere and are often unappreciated or even resented. So, we need to make sure our good intentions translate into affirmative action. Gordon B. Hinckley said: "My plea is that we stop seeking out the storms and enjoy more fully the sunlight. I am suggesting that as we go through life, we accentuate the positive. I am asking that we look a little deeper for the good, that we still our voices of insult and sarcasm, that we more generously compliment and endorse virtue and effort." (B.Y.U. Devotional, 10/1974).

"God does notice us, and He watches over us. But it is usually through another person that He meets our needs. Therefore, it is vital that we serve each other. The abundant life is achieved as we magnify our view of life, expand our appreciation of others, and recognize our own possibilities." (Spencer W. Kimball).

The more we follow the teachings of the Master, the more enlarged will our perspective become. We will recognize more opportunities for service that we would have otherwise seen without the magnifying lens of eternal perspective. We will find that "there is great security in spirituality, and we cannot have spirituality without service." (Spencer W. Kimball).

Traffic Islands Ahead

"The time
speedily cometh
that the Lord God shall
cause a great division among
the people, and the wicked
will he destroy; and he
will spare his people."
(2 Nephi 30:10).

When there are Traffic Islands Ahead that would separate Zion and Babylon into two separate and distinct camps, we should look to Zion for the source of truth.

Zion would say that the divine mind is the source of all knowledge, while Babylon would retreat to the secular humanist argument that man is its source. If we were to ask: "What is the ultimate reality?" Zion would answer that it is God, while Babylon would argue that it is the manifestation of natural law. If the question were: "What is the ultimate good? Zion would say it is whatever leads us to Christ, while Babylon would simply whine: "If it feels good, do it."

Zion will always be at odds with Babylon, for they are diametrically opposed in camps that are polarized at opposite ends of a very wide spectrum. There is really no common ground upon which meaningful dialogue may take place, because the foundations upon which Zion and Babylon rest are philosophically incompatible. The theology of Zion looks up to God for redemption, while Babylon looks no further than to the intellect for its salvation.

Babylon is so preoccupied with itself that, having eyes it cannot see. There is nothing out there that is interesting to those who are self-absorbed. Its inhabitants are wrapped up in themselves, and they make very small packages. Zion, however, is selflessly engaged because it is pure in heart, and sees with an eternal perspective. Babylon is distracted by carnal, sensual, and devilish enticements.

The faith of Zion is grounded in celestial surety, even as Babylon grovels in telestial tendencies. Zion gives full value, while Babylon takes what it can get. Zion stands for accountability, while Babylon shifts the blame in a flight from responsibility. Zion embraces the work ethic, while Babylon clamors for undeserved entitlements. Zion is spiritually mature, in contrast to Babylon's juvenile irresponsibility. Zion answers the call, while Babylon averts its eyes when the summons comes, thinks those who volunteer are suckers, and views service as a punishment.

Zion preaches repentance, while Babylon whines with rationalization for its sins, employs professional psychological apologists, and utilizes the lobbyist slogan: "The devil made me do it." Zion embodies substance while Babylon is transparent. Zion has a firm grasp on that which is real, while Babylon only grasps at straws in an illusion of reality that is of its own making. Zion deals in spiritual absolutes, while Babylon floats about in the vacuum of moral relativism. Zion has focus, while Babylon suffers from congenital short-sightedness. Zion is grounded upon the bedrock of principles, while Babylon confuses values for principles, and therefore basks in a false sense of security on a sandy foundation, thinking that all is well.

Zion listens, but Babylon talks. Zion is reflective, but Babylon is reactive. Zion looks for sanctuaries, while Babylon seeks soapboxes on the Hyde Park Corners of the Highways and Byways of Life. Zion has humility, but Babylon is prideful. Zion changes from the inside, while Babylon is changed from the outside. Zion acts, in a forum of free will, while Babylon is acted upon. Zion embraces freedom, but Babylon confuses license for freedom. Zion is focused on service, but Babylon is fixated by welfare.

Zion stands for something, while Babylon will fall for anything. Zion rededicates herself over altars in the temple, while Babylon argues its points over tables in the tavern. Zion exists to be taught, while Babylon exists to be told. Zion is proactive, while Babylon is reactive. Zion learns with her heart, while Babylon learns with its head. Zion has staying power, while Babylon has stalling power. Zion is temperate, while Babylon loses all sensibility in wanton gluttony. There are no poor in Zion, while the streets of Babylon are littered with beggars.

Zion relies upon the strength of the Lord, even as it unfurls its terrible banners, while Babylon rattles its sabers and mutters unsubstantiated threats. Zion understands consecration, even as Babylon is intent on desecration.

The Savior taught a great principle relating to the Traffic Islands that separate the people into two divisions on the Highways and Byways of Life. He said: "No man can serve two masters'; for either he will hate the one and love the other, or else he will hold to the one and despise the other." (3 Nephi 13:24). In the pre-mortal Council in Heaven, the Son of God came face to face with Traffic Islands. He and Michael put down a rebellion that would have wrecked the implementation of God's Plan. They knew that a house divided against itself cannot stand. (See Mark 3:25).

Zion cannot compromise its standards to become popular in Babylon, for then all hell would want to join it. We cannot hold membership in both the Church of God and the Great and Abominable Church of the Devil. We cannot live in Zion but have a summer home in Babylon. We cannot joy ride through Idumea, stopping along the way to sample its pleasures. The Traffic Islands that lie ahead, on the Highways and Byways of Life, give notice that Zion will always seeks higher ground, while Babylon is quite comfortable wallowing in the muddy marshes of mediocrity.

There is a basic instability associated with the hypocrisy of Babylon, and those who weave to the left of Traffic Islands will suffer eternally damaging consequences. They will be faced with conundrums of cosmic proportion. We are free to choose between Zion and Babylon but choose we must. We are free to follow the lifestyle of one or the other, but not both. That desire runs counter to the laws of nature and is fatally flawed. Those who pursue that path to the left of Traffic Islands will find themselves on a one-way road that leads to a personality precipice.

Disciples of Christ do not have the option to veer to the left of the Traffic Islands on the Highways and Byways of Life, to sample the pleasures of Babylon, to walk "in (their) own way, and after the image of (their) own god, whose image is in the likeness of the world, and whose substance is that of an idol." (D&C 1:16).

TRAIN DEPOT

Train Depot

The
strait and
narrow way of the
Highways and Byways
of Life has no shoulder
beckoning us to pull over,
turn off our engines, and
take a snooze, while the
world flies on by.

We all want to "hear the whistle sound, for those souls heaven bound." We are all eager to "climb onboard the glory ride and set our earthly bonds aside." Most assuredly, that "old train will leave some day, boarding Christians along the way." We can see it even now in our mind's eye, "roaring down those one-way tracks, and bound for heaven; it won't be back." We can hear the urgent call: "Get your ticket while you can. If you want a ride to Glory Land, we'll meet at the Lords' station. There's no time left for hesitation."

When we climb on board, there will be enough seats for all who want to experience the ride of their lives, because "this long black train has no gears. It's full throttle ahead leaving here." We'll be in good company, for "the archangel will be our engineer. We'll depart amidst angelic cheers." All Christians of conscience will soberly realize "the price of the ticket is paid for you. Jesus died on the cross for sins you do. Surrender to the Good Shepherd your all, before you miss that last boarding call." The promise is:

"We'll glide on the ride to heavens' shore, where we will endure troubles no more. So shed your shackles. There's no need to pack. Board that Glory Train with one-way tracks!" (Kenneth Ellison, "Glory Train").

Trucks & Heavy Vehicles: Balance Your Load

*We balance our
load on the Highways and
Byways of Life by being decided,
dogged, determined, indomitable,
resolute, untiring, and unwavering.
We are ardent, eager, fervent,
enthusiastic, passionate,
and zealous.*

As we make our way along the Highways and Byways of Life, it is readily apparent that it takes a great deal of effort to create balance, and very little inattention to allow chaos to reign unchecked. In fact, if we do not consciously focus on structure and stability, and exert ourselves to foster a sense of balance, everything tends to fall apart.

Even though they may seem to be at odds, however, inasmuch as they come from opposite ends of the behavioral spectrum, the laws of entropy and eternal progression must ultimately be in balance with each other. In fact, a healthy juxtaposition between opposing points of view is necessary for The Plan of Salvation to function smoothly. The perfect understanding by Jesus Christ of the concept of balance allowed Him to create our world and pronounce His efforts "very good." (Genesis 1:31). He has bound Himself to the Law of Eternal Progression, but it is as much defined by its opposites in the physical universe as it is by itself in heaven. (Se Moses 1:39). The presence of Satan in the Garden of Eden attests to that fact. (See Moses 4:6).

Disparity in the natural world is the consequence of imbalance, and its effects are inevitable unless the Author of Salvation intervenes by utilizing higher laws that trump such disproportion. As Paul perceptively explained to the Hebrews: "Ye have in heaven a better and an enduring substance." (Hebrews 10:34).

Our efforts to achieve and maintain equilibrium in our lives set the stage for the exercise of moral agency and dictate the implementation of other equally important and co-existing higher laws. Mercy, in particular, exists to mitigate the otherwise inevitable consequences of lives that are out of balance, and through Atonement facilitates our journey of progress in both time and eternity. The principles that make up The Plan of Salvation are the ultimate expression of balance.

Only if we incorporate into our lives the principles of The Plan can the disorder and destruction that result from imbalance be recognized, addressed, reversed, and erased with finality. Our obedience is consistent with the symmetry of heaven, while sin is harmful because it destroys our capacity to develop the steadiness that is representative of the Celestial Kingdom. The disorder of disobedience takes us further and further from the influence of the Spirit, whose purpose it is to guide us away from the precipice of destruction to a more secure sanctuary that abides the stability of higher laws.

To counteract the unsteadiness and lack of symmetry that naturally followed Adam and Eve's introduction into the telestial world, our days have been "prolonged, according to the will of God, that (we) might repent while in the flesh." (2 Nephi 2:21).

We now find ourselves on a journey through a lone and dreary world on the Highways and Byways of Life. Our five natural senses act as biological barometers that provide us with reliable measurements to gauge the pervasive and yet inexorable effects of imbalance that almost imperceptibly grind us down. Fortunately, we possess an innate urge to find the balance that is at the heart of the eternal laws that underpin The Plan of Salvation. As we come to understand its doctrines and principles, we discover within ourselves the capacity to move beyond the limitations of our everyday world.

Gradually, subtle extrasensory perceptions bring us to the realization that Gospel principles relating to the eternities supersede physical laws governing the temporal universe. We discover that there can be a reconciliation between the two when we are "born of God". Thereafter, our orientation is more to the expansive laws of eternity than to the restrictive confines of our physical world. When we establish harmony with heaven, we are in a better state of balance. We overcome the world with a freedom from incarceration to the inexorable imbalance of entropy.

(See 1 John 5:3). This independence is incalculable, indescribable, and inexplicable, and yet it is undeniable. It is not maturational, but is generational, as we become "new creatures in Christ."

As we travel the Highways and Byways of Life, we must be especially vigilant to make sure we Balance our Heavy Loads to kindle our faith, protect our testimonies, and save our souls.

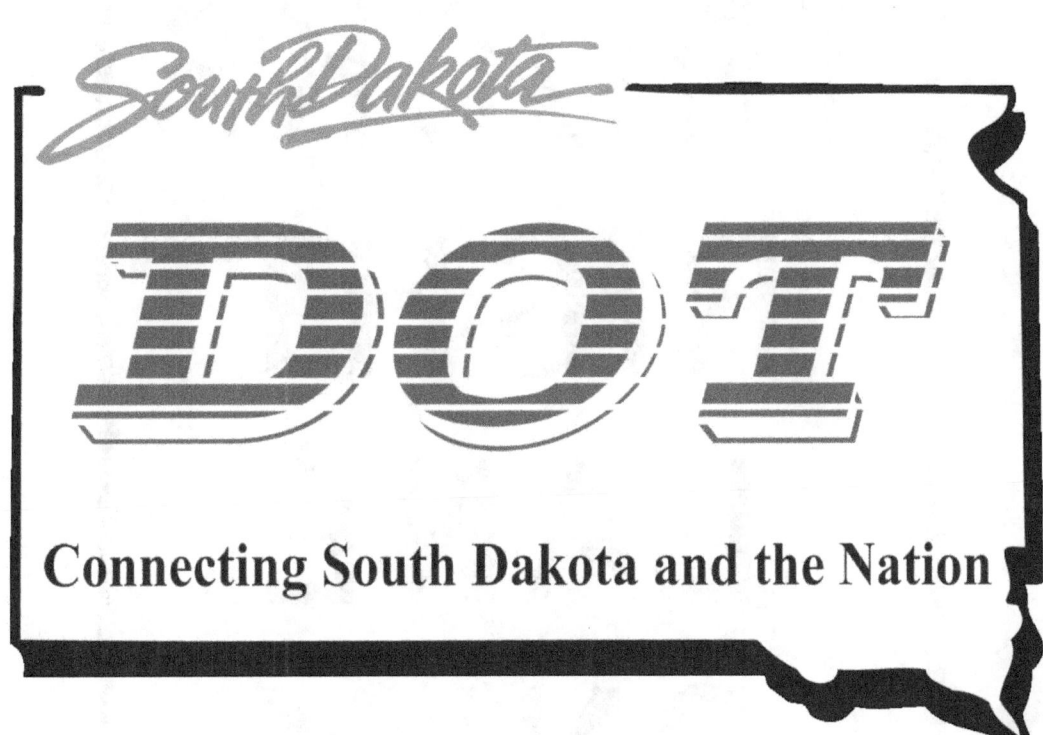

TRUCKS RIGHT LANE ONLY

Trucks: Right Lane Only

"Not enjoyment,
and not sorrow, is
our destined end or way;
but to act, that each tomorrow
finds us farther than today ... Lives
of great men all remind us that we can
make our lives sublime, and departing,
leave behind us footprints on the sands of
time. Let us then be up and doing, with a
heart for any fate; still achieving, still
pursuing. Learn to labor, and to
wait." (Longfellow).

Sometimes, those who carry the heaviest burdens are those who keep to the right, on the Highways and Byways of Life. As we plod along, we might only indirectly appreciate the eternities. However, by keeping to the right on the Highways and Byways of Life, even if we are heavily laden, "we can make our lives sublime, and departing, leave behind us footprints on the sands of time." It will be less likely that those footprints will be washed away by the incessant wave action of mortality that beats upon the roadbed. We need only to make sure that the tide in our affairs is taken at the flood, that it might lead on to fortune, and that the heavens might smile upon us and clothe us in the glory of God. (See Shakespeare, "Julius Caesar", Act 4, Scene 2).

Try your brakes

Try Your Brakes

The Highways
and Byways of Life
have many twists and turns
built into them that require us
to know how to use our brakes.
So, we had better make sure that
they are functioning properly
before we come up on the
next corner, as we most
certainly will.

How far you can dive into a corner on the Highways and Byways of Life before hitting your brakes, determines how fast you will come out onto the next straightaway.

Slowing down to negotiate corners efficiently is a skill that is only learned through practice. By using all of the available space on the road, you can come out of the turn faster, without losing control.

Interestingly, how you handle a corner depends upon what is on the road ahead of you afterwards. Your line will be different if there is a short straightaway, a long straightaway, or another series of turns. So it helps to know the road conditions, in your mind's eye.

The main reason to brake for a corner is to slow down just enough to clip the apex. If you come in too fast, you will take the turn wide, and if you slow down too much beforehand, you won't be able to exit the turn nearly as fast as you otherwise could have. Either way, you will unnecessarily scrub speed.

Braking early, and then accelerating through the corner can be a good strategy if you want to negotiate twists and turns like a pro. But whatever you do, make sure you slow down smoothly. Stomping on the brakes because you've misjudged the corner will upset the geometry of the turn, and it will cause you to lose your sense of balance and your feel for the road.

Trail-braking, or lightly braking into the turn before the apex, can help you to maintain a faster speed through the corner without sacrificing control. If you are distracted, have misjudged the turn, or have overzealously entered a corner too fast, recovery with trail-braking can help to keep you on the road. but locking up the brakes in panic when you realize you are out of your element is about the worst thing you can do.

When the Preacher wrote that "the race is not to the swift," he may have been saying that those who are best at handling the twists and turns of the Highways and Byways of Life know how to use not only the gas pedal, but also the brake pedal. They may have 1,000 horsepower under the hood, but they have learned how to tame the beast.

Because they have developed the habit to Try Their Brakes even before the need arises, they have ben blessed with staying power. They understand that life is not a sprint, but rather an endurance race. They do not run faster than they have strength, and they do not have the will to win so much as the will to prepare. Their proper prior preparation prevents poor performance when they need to brake for corners on the Highways and Byways of Life.

TURN ON HEADLIGHTS FOR SAFETY

Turn On Headlights For Safety

We need to be sure that
our headlights are on at all
times as we navigate the Highways
and Byways of Life, not only so that
others may see us, and stay clear,
but also that hidden obstacles
to our progression may be
clearly illuminated,
and thereby
avoided.

Joseph Smith, when asked how he could govern so many people, simply said: "I teach people correct principles, and they govern themselves." If we follow the covenant path with the way before us illuminated by faith, we can act independently within our sphere of influence and live life abundantly. This course entails risk, but it is God's ordained way. He explained to Adam while he was yet in the Garden: "Thou mayest choose for thyself, for it is given unto thee." (Moses 3:17). However, if we choose unwisely, carelessly, or thoughtlessly, if we do not drive with our headlights on for safety, we may forfeit our agency, and lose the freedom for which we have fought so hard, and at such a great cost.

Two Way Traffic

There are always two ways that lie before us. Which one we choose is up to us.

"Captivity" is mention 167 times in the scriptures. Particularly poignant is the counsel of Lehi to his son Jacob: "Men are free according to the flesh; and al things are given them which are expedient unto man. And they are free to choose liberty and eternal life, through the great Mediator of all men, or to choose captivity and death, according to the captivity and power of the devil." (2 Nephi 2:27).

"Young women of Scotland, life is before you", exhorted Helen Keller. "Two voices are calling you. One comes from the marsh of selfishness and force where success is won at any cost, and the other from the hilltops of justice and progress where even failure may ennoble. Two lights are on your horizon for you to choose. One is the fast-fading, will-o-the-wisp of power and materialism, the other the slowly rising sun of human brotherhood. Two laws stand today opposed, each demanding your allegiance. One is the law of death which daily invents new means of combat; this law obliges the nations to be ever at war. The other is the law of peace, of labour, of salvation, which strives to deliver man from the scourges which assail him. One looks only for violent conquest, the other for the relief of suffering humanity. Two ways lie open before you, one leading to a lower and yet lower plane of life, where are heard the weeping of the poor, the cries of little children, and the moans of pain, where manhood and womanhood shrivel, and possessions destroy the possessor; and the other leading to the highlands of the mind where are heard the glad shouts of humanity, and honest effort is rewarded with immortality." (Commencement Address to Queen Margaret College, Glasgow, Scotland, June 15, 1932, "Sightless but Seen; Deaf but Heard", p. 113).

There will always be Two Way Traffic on the Highways and Byways of Life, but those who are on Satan's payroll should not be difficult to spot. They falsely represent themselves. They write checks they cannot cash. There is no reserve in their tanks, which are running on empty. Their deceit is a reflection of their spiritual and moral bankruptcy. "Who shall ascend into the hill of the Lord", asked the Psalmist, "or who shall stand in his holy place? He that hath clean hands, and a pure heart, who hath not lifted up his soul unto vanity, nor sworn deceitfully." (Psalms 24:3-4).

Paul hoped that, in the Last Days, we would "henceforth be no more children, tossed to and fro, and carried about with every wind of doctrine, by the sleight of men, and cunning craftiness, whereby they lie in wait to deceive." (Ephesians 4:14). Elsewhere, he cautioned: "Beware lest any man spoil you through philosophy and vain deceit, after the tradition of men, after the rudiments of the world." (Colossians 2:8).

We must be on our guard, "for many deceivers are entered into the world." (2 John 1:7). "For there shall arise false Christs, and false prophets, and shall shew great signs and wonders, insomuch that, if it were possible, they shall deceive the very elect." (Matthew 24:24). But "the Lord shall deliver (us) from every evil work, and will preserve (us) unto his heavenly kingdom." (2 Timothy 4:18).

Under Construction

The Church
exists to build character
and its "auxiliary programs render
valuable assistance. But much of what
we do organizationally is scaffolding,
as we seek to build the individual,
and we must not mistake the
scaffolding for the soul."
(Harold B. Lee).

Much of what we do during our travels upon the Highways and Byways of Life is a process of construction. We are building our eternal identity. C.S. Lewis suggested: "Imagine yourself as a living house. God comes in to rebuild that house. At first, perhaps, you can understand what He is doing. He is getting the drains right and stopping the leaks in the roof, and so on. You knew that those jobs needed doing and so you are not surprised. But presently He starts knocking the house about in a way that hurts abominably and does not seem to make any sense. What on earth is He up to? The explanation is that He is building quite a different house from the one you thought of - throwing out a new wing here, putting on an extra floor there, running up towers, making courtyards. You thought you were being made into a decent little cottage, but He is building a palace." ("Mere Christianity").

As soon as we realize that we are works in progress, our pronoun problem will disappear. We will be far more prone to say "Thou" instead of "I." The Savior spoke of our potential that stems from interdependency, when He said that we may "become the sons of God, even one in me as I am one in the Father, as the Father is one in me, that we may be one." (D&C 35:2). Elsewhere, He clarified this unity: "Ye shall be even as I am, and I am even as the Father, and the Father and I are one." (3 Nephi 28:10).

We are much less likely to be critical of others when we realize that we are all Under Construction. Instead, we will work together, that we may fix our mistakes. We will measure twice and cut once. There will also be change-orders that need to be made, knowing that a house that has been fitly framed will grow into a temple unto the Lord. (See Ephesians 2:21).

His work is to perfect us, even if we are now only Under Construction. As Paul wrote: "He hath chosen us in him before the" pouring of the "foundation of the world, that we should be holy and without blame before him in love." (Ephesians 1:4).

Texas Department of Transportation

Uneven Lanes

The lanes on the
Highways and Byways of Life
are not all the same. Some are
rocky, some are twisty, some have
potholes, some go uphill most of
the way, and some are smooth
and straight. How we manage
the hand we were dealt can
have a profound effect
upon the quality of
our experiences.

"Two roads diverged in a yellow wood, and sorry I could not travel both and be one traveler, long I stood and looked down one as far as I could to where it bent in the undergrowth; Then took the other, as just as fair, and having perhaps the better claim, because it was grassy and wanted wear; though as for that the passing there had worn them really about the same, And both that morning equally lay in leaves no step had trodden black. Oh, I kept the first for another day! Yet knowing how way leads on to way, I doubted if I should ever come back. I shall be telling this with a sigh somewhere ages and ages hence: Two roads diverged in a wood, and I – I took the one less traveled by, and that has made all the difference." (Robert Frost, "The Road Not Taken").

Uneven Road Surface

Our
Heavenly Father
never said the road
surface of the Highways
and Byways of Life would
be smooth. In fact, he said
thru His prophet Lehi that there
would be bumps that would make
our teeth rattle. There must needs
be opposition in all things. In fact,
our human family has negotiated
Uneven Road Surfaces from
before the beginning
of time.

In September, 1823, the angel Moroni gave Joseph Smith the following counsel: "Wherever the sound (of the marvelous work) shall go" on the Highways and Byways of Life, "it shall cause the ears of men to tingle, and wherever it shall be proclaimed, the pure in heart shall rejoice, while those who draw near to God with their mouths, and honor him with their lips, while their hearts are far from him, will seek its overthrow, and the destruction of those by whose hand it is carried. Therefore, marvel not if your name is made a derision, and had as a byword among such," for the path I would have you follow will be a difficult one, accentuated by fallen trees, sticks and stones, washouts and soft shoulders, and other obstacles too numerous to mention. Just remember, especially when the going gets tough, that I have chosen you to be "the instrument in bringing (the glad message of the Restoration), by the gift of God, to the knowledge of the people." ("The Messenger and Advocate", 1:5, 2/1835).

According to his mother, Moroni also warned Joseph: "You are but a man. Therefore, you will have to be watchful and faithful to your trust, or you will be overpowered by wicked men" whose home turn is the Uneven Road Surface of the Highways and Byways of Life, "and if you do not take heed continually, they will succeed." (Lucy Mack Smith, "History of Joseph Smith", p. 110).

In spite of the unevenness of the road surface that led from Palmyra to Carthage, no unhallowed hand would be able to stop the work from progressing. Joseph was told: "Persecutions may rage, mobs may combine, armies may assemble, calumny may defame, but the truth of God will go forth boldly, nobly, and independent, till it has penetrated every continent, visited every clime, swept every country, and sounded in every ear, till the purposes of God shall be accomplished, and the Great Jehovah shall say the work is done" (H.C., 4:540).

Unplanned Detour

The roadmap of
life that we all follow
will present many seeming
detours. Some may actually turn
out to be the most direct route
to our envisioned destination,
while others will turn out
to be dead-ends, and
will need to be
avoided.

In a very real sense, each of us is confined to a world of our own making, and most of us are trapped within the narrowly defined perceptual prisons we have created for ourselves. Its walls are reinforced with the razor-wire of limiting beliefs, those stories we tell ourselves that cause us to sabotage our own best efforts. They can damage and even cripple the conduct of our lives, diminish our abilities, compromise our progress, and prevent us from reaching our goals. Although all of us have limiting beliefs, everyone has the power to neutralize them. Most people, however, don't realize it's possible, and for that matter, aren't even aware that they have made conscious decisions about the direction they have chosen to go.

When we are confronted by Unplanned Detours on the Highways and Byways of Life, we need to consult our most trusted Trip Advisor to help us to determine which way is the right way to go.

Viewpoint Ahead

The Highways
and Byways of Life are
dotted with flower festooned
roadside stands that serve a wide
variety of refreshment. With what we
choose to rejuvenate our bodies,
minds and spirits depends
entirely upon our
Viewpoint.

We are reminded of Dag Hammarskjöld's observation: "The longest journey is the journey inward, for he who has chosen his destiny has started upon a quest for the source of his being."

Some people grumble that roses have thorns, while others are thankful that thorns have roses. Faced with adversity, some see only a sour lemon, while others give thanks that they have been given the means to make lemonade. When served a refreshing cold drink, some see the glass as half empty, while others see it as half full. When they look to the right, to the left, and even above, some conclude that God is no where to be found, while others believe that He is now here, and can be found.

Sometimes, it seems that positive energy comes in discrete packages that are dispensed by especially cheerful individuals who always have a smile on their face and a spring in their step. For example, think of those who have the amazing ability to light up the room by their mere presence. Think of charismatic leaders who inspire their followers to defy the odds and attempt the impossible, of those whose compelling charm and magnetic personalities have an almost mystical draw, of those who can so easily captivate others with the power of their rhetoric, of those with the hypnotic ability to mesmerize their listeners with magical word-portraits that are motivational and inspiring, and of the natural appeal and irresistible draw of those whose minds and spirits have been endowed with insight, intuition, inspiration, discernment, and revelation, and whose lips have been kissed with honey and touched by the finger of God.

These people, who have been blessed with a celestial point of view, have dedicated themselves to worthwhile activities that give their lives meaning and purpose. They are committed to self-improvement and engagement with others, in ways that are mutually supportive. They welcome constructive criticism and do not waste time being defensive. They share their knowledge and ideas with others, and are mentors to those who follow them on the path toward self-actualization. They enjoy the journey as much as the destination. They do not allow power and influence to corrupt them or to deter them from focusing their energies on core principles. Even when life throws them a curve, they smile. realize that happiness is contagious, and as carriers, they infect others with their cheerfulness. They are courteous and thoughtful, and they speak of others as if their parrot were the town gossip. They are kind and gentle, especially when interacting with the village idiot. When necessity arises, they use diplomacy, celebrating the differences between themselves and others, because they know that we are all children of God, with talents and abilities to share with each other.

Vision Just Ahead

The scope of God's kingdoms is beyond our comprehension as we travel the Highways and Byways of Life, but prophetic insight provides greater clarity.

Joseph Smith said: "The great Jehovah contemplated the whole of the events connected with the earth pertaining to the plan of salvation, before it rolled into existence, or ever the morning stars sang together for joy; the past, the present, and the future were and are, with him, one eternal 'now.'" (Teachings", p. 220).

The Savior exists in the present tense. His "course is one eternal round, the same today as yesterday, and forever" that allows him to see from multiple perspectives in time, "the beginning and the end." (D&C 35:1). As Alma explained to Corianton: "All is as one day with God, and time only is measured unto men." (Alma 40:8). Einstein was correct; time is relative.

Our destiny was prepared in the pre-earth existence, has been molded in mortality, and will be established in eternity, when the angels will warmly smile upon us. The trajectory of our ascent to heaven's gate leaves us heavy with anticipation that the Vision Just Ahead, on the Highways and Byways of Life, will be breathtaking in its scope and brilliance.

Visitor Information

As we travel the Highways and Byways of Life, it slowly dawns upon us that the itinerary God has outlined for us will eventually lead us to "that undiscovered country from whose bourn no traveler returns." ("Hamlet").

Like the knight, the squire, the prioress, the nun, the monk, the friar, the merchant, the clerk, the cook, the miller, the parson, the plowman, the physician, and the other 15 main characters in Chaucer's "Canterbury Tales", we are all in the same boat, so to speak. We all need a Tour Guide, who will take care of us during our journey.

Who are these visitors who have booked passage on the pale blue dot we call planet Earth? They are those who speak Aymara, Afrikaans, Fijian, Polish, Mandarin, and around 6,500 other languages. They live in 196 countries on 7 continents and on the isles of the sea. The color of their skin is red, yellow, brown, black, white, and everything in between. They are equally comfortable wearing a sarong, a grass skirt, a lava lava, a burqa, a tupeno, or blue jeans. They find shelter in igloos, bamboo huts, thatch cottages, canvas tents, cardboard shanties, and condominiums.

They eat kaeng khua, poi, muamba de galinha, raggmunk, hrútspungar, and hamburgers on sesame seed buns. Most importantly, and whether or not they recognize the feeling, each one carries within their heart a spark of divinity that is the warm glow of the light of Christ.

**WARNING
AVALANCHE
AREA**
NO STOPPING
ON ROADWAY

Warning: Avalanche Area

*If we
do not choose to
follow the Savior, we
have implicitly chosen to
follow another path, upon
which we will stand a good
chance of being blind-sided
by the Destroyer.*

We have all witnessed the spectacle of those who "have been once enlightened by the Spirit of God, and (who) have had great knowledge of things pertaining to righteousness, and then have fallen away into sin and transgression. They become more hardened, and thus their state becomes worse than though they had never known these things." (Alma 24:30).

Joseph Fielding Smith, Jr. taught: "Before you joined the Church you stood on neutral ground. When the Gospel was preached, good and evil were set before you. You could choose either or neither. There were two opposite masters inviting you to serve them. You left the neutral ground and you can never get back on to it. Should you forsake the Master you enlisted to serve, it will be by the instigation of the evil one, and you will follow his dictation and be his servant." (C.E.S. Manual, p. 258). You will enter the Avalanche

Area of the Adversary and risk being buried in a telestial terrain trap under tons of sin.

During the 40-year sojourn of Israel on the Highways and Byways of Life, Moses had given them God's law, acted as His spokesperson, and served as their guide. He was the only leader an entire generation of Israelites had known. But the Lord took him at the end of their journey, just when they faced their greatest tests. His contingency plan was to call Joshua to succeed Moses and to command him to be strong, have courage, study the scriptures, and be obedient. (See Joshua 1:6). Joshua rose to the occasion as he allowed God to shape his nature. Similarly, as we allow God to shape our character, we can develop divine attributes and accomplish the things He wants us to do.

Our own opportunities for growth require strength and moral courage. Each of us has 168 hours each week, much of it discretionary time to do with as we please. Only 2 hours are spent in Church. We need to ask ourselves: How many hours are spent hanging out, watching TV., playing video games, or on our computers or our mobile devices?

Perhaps we should budget our time as carefully as we budget our money. Concentrating on the things that really matter endows us with a special power to manage the gift of time. We learn to take time with discipline, find time with care, spend time with thoughtfulness, invest time with wisdom, share time with pleasure, and even make time with diligence. Turning our attention to the weightier matters of the law gives us a sense of independence, as we learn something new every day. It can open our hearts and our minds to the breathtaking expansion of understanding. As we practice a learning style that embraces the Spirit, we will discover a pattern that will become our norm.

Warning I Do Dumb Things

Knowing that we all do dumb things, Brigham Young said that "the first principle that ought to occupy our attention, and which is the mainspring of all action, is the principle of improvement." The Holy Ghost overlooks our faults and foibles, and helps us to constantly strive to do more, to be better, to seek knowledge and wisdom; to emulate the Olympic motto "Citius, Altius, Fortius", or "Faster, Higher, Stronger."

Upon the Highways and Byways of Life, even though we Do Dumb Things, if we learn from our mistakes through repentance, we will be doubly blessed with happiness now and the certain promise of joy in our Father's Kingdom. If we ask Him, He will do everything within His power to help us, as any parent would. But He has special abilities in this regard. He can give us "revelation upon revelation, knowledge upon knowledge, that (we might) know the mysteries and peaceable things - that which bringeth joy, that which bringeth life eternal. (D&C 42:61).

Obstacles are those frightful demons we see when our minds and our spirits wander far from Home. They loom large with a gratuitous significance. Thru the Holy Ghost, our Father gives us the vision to see beyond potential stumbling blocks and then to creativity turn them into stepping-stones that pave the way to higher achievement. Our Father, His Son Jesus Christ, and the Holy Ghost all know that we are going to Do Dumb Things, but They allow us to do them anyway. But they also bless us to see things as they could be, and then They enlighten us with the tools we need to work with all our means to rewrite our personal history. Our desire to change "generates power, for a mind once stretched by a new idea never returns to its original dimension." (Oliver Wendell Holmes).

We are beings of light who now find ourselves traveling the Highways and Byways of Life. We come from a more exalted sphere, "with glory trailing from our feet, and endless promise in our eyes." ("Saturday's Warrior"). But we have forgotten all, including the memory of our former life and the purpose of our call. As we figure out who we really are, we will Do Dumb Things, but our Savior and the Holy Ghost will never forsake us. Sooner or later, the light will gather in the east, and it will finally dawn on us that there is something out there that is worth fighting for; something that lies just beyond the hills of time. Without the spark of divinity that compels us to discover why we're here and where we are going, we grow old before our time.

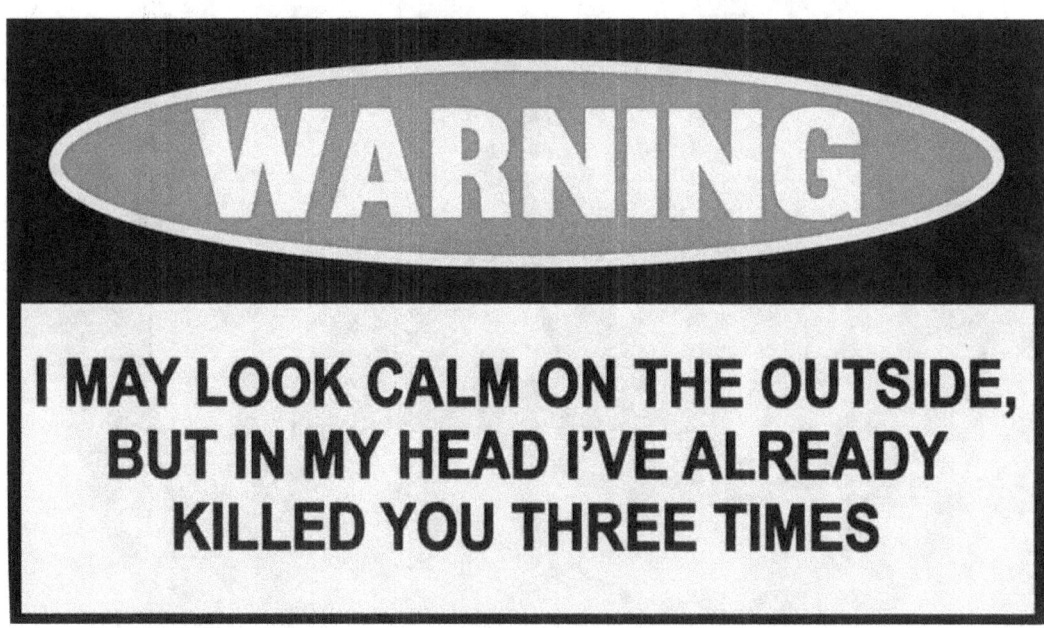

Warning:
I May Look Calm

> A puckish
> observation
> is that revenge
> is a dish that is best
> served cold, when we are
> no longer caught up in the
> heat of the moment, but think
> that we can afford to be crafty,
> cunning, and calculating as we plot
> our payback. But that strategy is like
> swallowing poison and hoping it will
> kill the other guy. Our repentance,
> and the Savior's forgiveness,
> don't work that way.

At some point, during our journey along the Highways and Byways of Life, we need to encounter the Atonement, because only our understanding of the grace of God and forgiveness through repentance allows us to overcome our selfish and morally indefensible desire for personal justice without mercy.

Desperation was really at the root of Lucifer's alternative proposal at the Council, when he boasted: "I will redeem all mankind, that one soul shall not be lost." (Moses 4:1). He exhibited his true colors with that revealing assertion. Because he was incapable of forgiveness, the thought of remembering no more the sins of his repentant brethren scared the living daylights out of him. Even then, the noble and principled qualities that were expressed in the Atonement stood in sharp contrast to the damning character flaws of the morning star who lacked staying power, and so, Lucifer fell from heaven with a deafening roar, and a thud whose reverberations are felt even today. (See Revelation 9:1).

Lucifer became Satan because of his unprincipled and unilaterally dogmatic posturing; because he could not wrap his mind around the concept of forgiveness. He would have had us believe that his counterfeit proposal could simply ignore correction because there would be no need for propitiation.

The keystone of The Plan of Salvation is the Atonement that looks directly into the jaws of spiritual death without averting its eyes. It was not the Savior, but the Devil who was the first to blink, and so, he was cast out of heaven. It is he who will not support his children as they journey on, along the Highways and Byways of Life. (See Alma 30:44). Let us never forget that the Devil may look calm, but in his head, he has already killed us three times. (First, during his rebellion after the Council, then here on earth, and finally at the Last Judgment). Our Savior is here to make sure that doesn't become a self-fulfilling prophecy.

WARP DR

Warp Drive

> We travel along the
> Highways and Byways of Life
> at a speed that is consistent with
> the road conditions. But what
> happens when we take the
> exit to eternity, and
> those conditions
> change?

The physics behind "Warp Drive" engines may help to explain how to surmount the problem of exceeding the cosmic speed limit, when we have exited the highway at the second star on the right, and have sailed on 'til the morning of the first day of the rest of our life. In the Star Trek Universe, when a ship goes to warp, it is able to move through the observable universe at speeds faster than the speed of light because time has been warped. The ship has taken advantage of the curvature of spacetime to get from point A to point B at a velocity faster than the speed of light, because the distance between those two points is no longer a straight line.

But do we really need to worry about mastering Warp Drive, or might it be better to acknowledge that the omniscience, omnipotence and even omnipresence of God will take care of the problem by themselves? Soon enough, we will live in eternity, when time (and these questions) will become insignificant. Then, we will better comprehend the expressions "Alpha and Omega", the "Beginning and the End", and "I Am that I am."

When we move on past mortality, time will cease to exist, and we will no longer have the need to wear wristwatches. "See you later!" and "Have a good day!" will no longer be in our vocabulary. For that matter, listlessness, boredom, monotony, and ennui will be alien to our experience. We will be up, and about, and moving. As did Joseph Smith, we will exclaim: "O Lord God Almighty, maker of heaven, earth, and seas, and of all things that in them are ... let thy pavilion be taken up; let thy hiding place no longer be covered." (D&C 121:4).

When we move into eternity, we will surely discover that any of a number of possible scenarios will exist. We may find that time was the source of our weariness. On the other hand, we may discover that it was the quixotic element of time that sparked and sustained our interest in life. We may expand Lehi's grand exposition on opposition to encompass both the positive and negative aspects of time. Only time will tell.

When we have overcome all things, and we are finally released from the time constraints that now hinder our progress, enthusiasm and fervor might become our natural passions. It may dawn on us that eternal progression is largely concerned with shedding self-limiting and finite constraints of time from the unending equations that stimulate growth and development, define improvement, and permit progress.

We may find that mortality, with the arrow of time moving relentlessly, inexorably, and unremittingly forward in one direction only, was not our natural dimension. We may then see with greater clarity that it is from Kolob that the order of the creations of God are spatially and temporally governed, and it is from there that the boundaries of heaven are established beyond the reach of detection by even the most sophisticated instruments utilized by terrestrial scientists. The Hubble Space Telescope can see 14 billion light years into our past, almost back to the moment of creation at the Big Bang, but it cannot gaze into heaven five minutes. If we could do that, we "would know more than (we) would by reading all that has ever been written on the subject." (Joseph Smith, H.C. 6:50).

We may recognize that we were never entirely comfortable in our mortal circumstances. We may realize that Heavenly Father created time itself as a steady and methodical taskmaster that could dispassionately motivate us to move forward without His overt encouragement. Could it be that, when we lived by faith, it was time that we had to thank? When we have overcome all things, and we are completely reconciled unto Christ, will we no longer depend upon the emotional crutch of time? Will we find that we were "never really at home in time?" asked Neal A. Maxwell.

He wondered why it is that we now "find ourselves impatiently wishing to hasten the passage of time, or to hold back the dawn. We can do neither, of course ... because we belong to eternity. Time, as much as any one thing, whispers to us that we are strangers here." ("B.Y.U. Speeches of The Year", 1979). Warp Drive. Bring it on!

Warp Drive? Eternity engines driven by priesthood power? Celestial catalytic converters? The fuel additive of faith? All we know for sure is that "zero hour is 9 a.m. and we're gonna be as high as a kite by then ... on such a timeless flight ... I'm a rocket man!" ("Rocket Man. I think its gonna to be a long, long time", song by Elton John and lyrics by Bernie Taupin).

Watch Downhill Speed

*Our downhill speed, when
we have exited the Highways and
Byways of Life, may be governed by
certain bounds and conditions that
are specifically tailored to the
then-existing environment.*

Heavenly Father explained it this way: "There are many kingdoms, for there is no space in the which there is no kingdom, and there is no kingdom in which there is no space, either a greater or a lesser kingdom. And unto every kingdom is given a law; and unto every law there are certain bounds also and conditions." (D&C 88:37-38).

When Jehovah stood in the presence of God the Father at the time of the creation of the earth, He said to those assembled: "We will go down, for there is space there, and we will take of these materials, and we will make an earth." (Abraham 3:24). The space reserved for the earth already existed; all that was necessary was for Jehovah to "go" there and establish, or set in motion, the laws, bounds and conditions by which it could exist as a temporal entity in the three-dimensional space and one-dimensional time matrix that is our present reality. As Luke wrote, God "made the world and all things therein ... and hath determined the times ... and the bounds of their habitation." (Acts 17:24 &

26). He established both the spatial and temporal conditions that would define the rules of the road on the Highways and Byways of Life. He established the cosmic speed limit that would at first calibrate and then govern our existence, but He inserted a codicil. Eternal progression would have temporal and spatial parameters that allow Him, and that would one day allow us, to exceed the speed limit.

We are generally locked on telestial targets and content ourselves with a rev-limiter on the power plant that fuels both light bulbs and stars. This governor limits both the output of photons and our acceleration to 186,282 miles (300,000,000 meters) per second. We are drawn to the light as moths are drawn to fire, and we generally flutter about without purpose or direction. In other words, higher-level thinking is often beyond the reach of our comprehension.

For "my thoughts are not your thoughts", the Lord reminded us. "Neither are your ways my ways ... For as the heavens are higher than the earth, so are my ways higher than your ways, and my thoughts than your thoughts." (Isaiah 55:8-9). We will never understand the physical universe so completely that we will become its master. We cannot hope to substitute our intellect for that of God. We can never, in any significant way, understand the eternities while we remain mired in the physical world. Well did the Psalmist counsel: "Be still, and know that I am God." (Psalms 46:10). For now, we need to obey the speed limit, especially when we are going downhill. It provides us with order and gives us peace of mind.

But "great and marvelous are the works of the Lord",

Jacob exclaimed. "How unsearchable are the depths of the mysteries of him; and it is impossible that man should find out all his ways. And no man knoweth of his ways save it be revealed unto him." (Jacob 4:8). "O the vainness, and the frailties, and the foolishness of men!" wrote Lehi. For "when the are learned, they think they are wise" and they suppose "they know of themselves, wherefore, their wisdom is foolishness and it profiteth them not." (2 Nephi 9:28-29).

As Paul cautioned the Colossian Saints: "Beware lest any man spoil you through philosophy and vain deceit, after the tradition of men, after the rudiments of the world." (Colossians 2:8). 'We don't understand how God accomplishes the trick of moving about His universe without regard to the cosmic speed limit (the speed of light), but we know that at that velocity matter turns into pure energy. Because $E = MC^2$, (energy equals mass times the speed of light squared), E is a very large number, indeed! So, if you were traveling very near the speed of light, it would take a tremendous amount of energy to increase your speed by just a few feet per second. This also means it would take an infinite amount of energy to travel at the speed of light. This is why "Spaceballs", the motion picture spoof on "Star Wars", utilized "Ridiculous Speed", and "Ludicrous Speed."

Intriguingly, Paul explained that when God raised His Son from the dead, He "set Him at His own right hand in the heavenly places, far above all principality, and power, and might, and dominion." (Ephesians 1:20-21). Let's just say that God had energy sufficient to the task, for with Him "all things are possible." (Matthew 19:26).

Watch For Congestion Ahead

Bad things happen to good people, and even the righteous struggle. But, because of the Atonement, they do not need to suffer the consequences that are related to poor choices, or to unresolved sin.

All of us will experience Congestion Ahead, on the Highways and Byways of Life. The trick is to go with the flow, and not allow ourselves to be worn down by the vicissitudes of life. It has been said that nothing can dim the light that shines from within; that we do not need magic to transform the word, for we have all the power we need within ourselves; that although we must accept finite disappointment, we must never lose infinite hope; it might be necessary to let go of the life we have planned, in order to enjoy the life that is waiting for us; nothing is impossible - in fact I'm possible; the perfect moment is the one you are in now; the past does not determine the future unless you live there; and finally, your crown has been bought and paid for - put it on and wear it.

Watch For Emergency Vehicles

There will be
times and circumstances
when we will see the spiritual
equivalents of red, white, and
blue strobe lights in our rear
view mirrors, as we plod
along the Highways and
Byways of Life.

If we pull over at such times, the proverbial police car or the archetypal ambulance might just ignore us and whiz by, allowing us to avoid interfering with the management of the emergencies that are a part of life. If the situation involves us, however, by interacting calmly and cooperatively with the authorities who demand our undivided attention, our chances of a successful resolution to the problem will improve.

The Savior interacts with us under two distinct scenarios: when things are going well, and when thing are not going well. Longfellow memorably wrote about the footprints that we leave behind on the sands of time. Sometimes, however, there are two sets of footprints, one His and one ours, as we walk together, but during times of particular difficulty, there may be only one. Of course, it is during those trying times that the Savior lifts us onto his shoulders. We are comforted that He will lead us out of the bondage of ignorance "by power, and with a stretched-out arm." (D&C 103:17). The very fact that He is "mighty to save" suggests that we must allow Him to become involved in our lives, so He may rescue us from our follies. (2 Nephi 31:19).

As we make our way along the Highways and Byways of Life, we need to recognize that it might just be the Savior Who is at the wheel of the emergency vehicle that we see in the rear-view mirror, and that its flashing lights are His message that it is we who need His immediate attention.

Watch For Farm Machinery

Farm Machinery on the Highways and Byways of Life reminds us that it is probably no coincidence that Adam and Eve were commanded to till the ground, and that it was ordained that it would be by the sweat of their brow that they were to eke out their existence.
(See Genesis 3:19).

Agriculture and animal husbandry have been the norm for most of the travelers on the Highways and Byways of Life throughout recorded history, and it has generally been an exhausting undertaking for both farmers and ranchers.

Nevertheless, farming is literally the ordained way to make a living. Before the foundation of the world as we know it, "the Lord God took the man, and put him into the Garden of Eden to dress it and to keep it." (Genesis 2:15). And then, when Adam and Eve were driven from the Garden, he was told: By "the sweat of thy face shalt thou eat bread, till thou return unto the ground; for out of it wast thou taken: for dust thou art, and unto dust shalt thou return." (Genesis 3:19).

Of such manual labor, Ernest L. Wilkinson declared: "I want to bear you my testimony that if you develop the habit of work, it will be the most invigorating, satisfying, even relaxing and greatest blessing of your life. The opportunity to work is God's greatest blessing to mankind, and this means six days of each week." Neal A. Maxwell called work a spiritual necessity and counseled that we avoid it at peril to our souls. A favorite saying of Harold B. Lee was: "Work without vision is drudgery. Vision without work is dreamery. But work with vision is destiny."

Make no small plans", declared Daniel Burnham, "for they have no magic to stir men's souls." "Cease to be idle; cease to be unclean; cease to find fault one with another; cease to sleep longer than is needful; retire to thy bed early, that ye may not be weary; arise early, that your bodies and your minds may be invigorated." (D&C 88:124). The Lord wants us to think big, as we put our minds, our bodies, and our spirits to work.

Watch For Oncoming Traffic

*The light
we see at the
end of the tunnel
could be the headlamp
of an approaching train.
But it might instead signal
the gathering light of a new
day. Which it turns out to
be largely depends
upon us.*

Sometimes, a "no" comes as the answer to the "specifications set forth in our petitions." (Neal A. Maxwell). We need to let go, and let God, even as we Watch For Oncoming Traffic. We express thanks for our Father's greater vision and prepare ourselves for negative responses. We learn from them as much as we do from affirmations, for we know that whom the Lord loves, He also chastens. (See D&C 95:1). When we receive a bouquet of roses as the answer to our prayers, we accept the thorns as well as the buds. Some people grumble about those thorns. We try to maintain our perspective, to be thankful that thorns have roses.

Watch For Pedestrians

*If we want to have
the greatest success in life,
we must kneel at the feet of
Jesus because His footprints
have changed the course
of history.*

Pedestrians have always played an important part of our navigation along the Highways and Byways of Life, and none is greater than the Savior of the world. He never strayed more than a hundred miles or so from His birthplace, and except for the one time that He entered Jerusalem on the back of a donkey (in fulfillment of prophecy), He went everywhere on foot. He was the quintessential Pedestrian. Today, we undertake pilgrimages at great effort and expense just to retrace His footsteps; to share, in a small way, the bonds of common experience.

"I walked today where Jesus walked, in days of long ago. I wandered down each path He knew, with reverent step and slow. Those little lanes, they have not changed; a sweet peace fills the air. I walked today where Jesus walked, and felt His presence there. My pathway led through Bethlehem, its memory ever sweet. The little hills of Galilee, that knew His childish feet. The Mount of Olives; hallowed scenes that Jesus knew before. I saw the mighty Jordan row, as in the days of yore. I knelt today where Jesus knelt, where all alone he prayed. The Garden of Gethsemane; my heart felt unafraid. I picked my heavy burden up, and with Him at my side, I climbed the Hill of Calvary where on the Cross He died. I walked today where Jesus walked, and felt Him close to me." (Daniel Twohig).

The feet are very sensitive. Helen Keller once gave a speech, and at its conclusion the crowd gave her a thunderous round of applause. When asked how she knew what the reaction of the audience had been, she said she felt their appreciation through the vibrations in her feet. This sheds light on the statement of the Prophet Joseph Smith, who said after receiving revelation: "My whole body was full of light, and I could see even out at the ends of my fingers and toes." (N. B. Lundwall, "The Vision", p. 11, see Proverbs 6:13).

Perhaps this is why the angel Moroni hovered in the air during his first visit to the boy prophet in his bedchamber. He wanted to see better, for he could see even out of his toes. We know for certain that if our bodies are single to the glory of God, our "whole bodies shall be filled with light, and there shall be no darkness in (us); and that body which is filled with light comprehendeth all things." (D&C 88:67).

When the Savior said: "Go ye into all the world and preach the Gospel" the command could only be carried out with the feet. (Mark 16:15). Isaiah recognized this, writing: "How beautiful upon the mountains are the feet of him that bringeth good tidings, that publisheth peace; that bringeth good tidings of good, that publisheth salvation." (Isaiah 57:2).

There are over 100 references in the Gospels to His walking. We cannot ponder the significance of His ministry without a conscious appreciation of His feet. His most basic invitations: "Come, follow me", and "Go ye into all the world", indirectly reference our feet. (Luke 18:22 & Mark 16:15). Ultimately, it will be our feet that take us to kneel before Him, at His feet.

In the scriptures, many parts of the human anatomy have been related to behavior, both in metaphor and simile. We read of the foot of pride, and the foot of Israel; feet that are offensive, that are as pillars of fire, that are like fine brass, like the sole of a calf, as iron and clay, and that are shod with the preparation of the gospel of peace. When President Spencer W. Kimball said: "I am like an old shoe, to be worn out in the service of the Lord", he was utilizing the vivid imagery of feet, and that is something to which we can all relate.

Watch For School Bus

Making
good choices very subtly
increases our power to make
even more of them. If we look
very carefully during our travels,
we will discover that it is the Holy
Ghost Who guides the school bus
that picks us up and threads
its way along the Highways
and Byways, with many
stops at the learning
laboratories of
life.

The most powerful weapons used in modern warfare, and the most coldly efficient ways to take life, utilize chemical, nuclear, and biological agents. But the most diabolical way to neutralize the influence of the Holy Ghost and kill "the candle of the Lord" is through the manipulation of ideology. (Proverbs 20:27).

Agency is the lynchpin of The Plan of Salvation. Although its righteous application is fundamental to the operation of The Plan, it remains a difficult concept to master. But here's the really amazing thing about free will: The more it is exercised with responsibility, the more of it there is to use, and when it is used wisely, the Holy Ghost moves right in to confirm the validity of our righteous choices and to establish a habit pattern. The less wisely it is used, the less of it there is to use, as the Holy Ghost, the bearer of all truth, withdraws.

Failing to board the School Bus when it stops to pick us up limits our choices and subsequently hobbles our freedom to make good choices. Anyone who has suffered the consequences of bad choices knows firsthand, with chilling certainty, what it means to be snared in Satan's strong cords and feel the downward drag of the weight of the chains of hell.

The kicker is that we can employ the very principle Satan uses to get us to follow him instead of the school bus, to withstand His temptations and to hearken to the voice of the Spirit. The correct application of the highest expression of free will, which is moral agency, can be used to set us free from enslavement to satanically self-defeating behaviors. At the end of the day, agency is both the beginning and the end of The Plan., and the tenet around which revolves the grand principle of opposition in all things.

Finally, the Judgment will hinge upon whether or not we boarded the bus. The Holy Ghost will be at the Judgment Bar to testify if we were true to our moral center, or if we let our spiritual compass spin wildly out of control because we turned our backs on the promptings that had been so freely given. Climbing aboard that School Bus, it would seem, pays big dividends at the end of the day.

Watch For Wildlife

All around us, the world is self-absorbed in partying, as if there were no tomorrow. Its hedonistic philosophy is: "Eat, drink, and be merry, for tomorrow we die."
(2 Nephi 28:7).

The world's party-goers simply do not recognize the value of nourishment from the good word of God. Instead, they embrace the fleeting stimulation of artificial sweeteners, the empty calories of convenience, and the hypoglycemia of hypocrisy. They jostles to and fro on a platform of platitudes while they wait to board the Excess Express in a vain search for a shortcut to perfection. But the day will come when they will look in the mirror and see themselves for who they really are: Spiritual bodies that have become "one sorry sight! No more than skeletons, covered with skin, who will get up to heaven, but never get in. 'Another soul's mine!' they will hear Satan scream. 'Give man something nice, and he'll take the extreme!' OK, I'll admit it; I'll outright confess. For the fast way to hell, take the Excess Express." (Anonymous).

In our own pre-mortal life, there were surely family

gatherings but no wild frat parties. We must have recognized that strenuous spiritual exercise would give us vigorous vitality and leave us stronger, and so we surely learned to use our recovery time wisely. We must have developed the capacity to carefully monitor our bodies' vital signs; to feel the spiritual equivalents of oxygen-debt and lactic acid buildup; to monitor the efforts of our minds to keep pace with our spiritual development. We surely experienced brief bursts of energy resulting in spectacular achievement, but more importantly, we must have discovered that sustained effort would carry us further along the road leading to eternal life. In that setting, we must have also learned the value of developing endurance, so that when the time would come to go the second mile, instead of embracing the carefree lifestyle of the rich and famous, it would be easier to put our nose to the grind-stone, simply because of the force of habit.

We Watch for Wildlife on the Highways and Byways of Life because we don't want to be caught on the Religious Roundabouts (see above) upon which hedonistic thrill-seekers have strayed, causing their heads to spin in confusion.

Wedding Season Ahead

Love is in the air
all along the Highways and
Byways of Life. Fortunately,
marriage is ordained of God,
and weddings are always
in season.

"The bride and groom are about to proclaim 'I love you' before the world. Three little words. And say 'I do.' Three little letters. It's the simplest part of the day; but there is nothing simple about the things that will remain unsaid. 'I do' means I do know I could be hurt, but I am ready to be healed with you. It means I do want to try, even when the fear of failure tugs at me to hold me back. I do not know the future, but I am ready to be surprised with you along the way. 'I do' means I do want your love and I do give you mine. Nothing we do in life will ever be the same, because we will be doing it all together." (Anonymous).

WEIGH STATION ↗

Weigh Station

"Let me be weighed in an even balance, that God may know mine integrity." (Job 31:6). (See Daniel 5:27).

President David O. McKay made the following statement to a Group of brethren from the Physical Facilities Department of the Church, who had gathered at his Hotel Utah apartment, in June 1965. According to one of the brethren present, he said: "Let me assure you, brethren, that some day you will have a personal priesthood interview with the Savior, Himself. If you are interested, I will tell you the order in which He will ask you to account for your earthly responsibilities. First, He will request an accountability report about your relationship with your wife.

Second, He will ... request information about your relationship to each and every child. Third, he will want to know what you have personally done with the talents you were given in the premortal existence. Fourth, He will want a summary of your activity in your Church assignments. Fifth ... if you were honest in all your dealings. Sixth, He will ask for an accountability report on what you have done to contribute in a positive manner to your community, state, country and the world."

Weight Restriction Notice

When
the crosses
we carry seem too
heavy for us to bear,
we are fortunate if along
the Highways and Byways of
Life we discover that there is One
Who can promise, with unfaltering
certainty, that if we take upon
ourselves His yoke, it will be
easy, and our burdens
will be light.

"How sweet is the sound of Amazing Grace that saved a wretch like me! I once was lost, but now am found; was blind, but now I see. 'Twas grace that taught my heart to fear and grace my fears relieved; how precious did that grace appear, the hour I first believed! Through many dangers, toils, and snares, I have already come. 'Tis grace has brought me safe thus far, and grace will lead me home.

The Lord has promised good to me, His word my hope secures. He will my shield and portion be, as long as life endures. Yes, when this flesh and heart shall fail, and mortal life shall cease, I shall possess, within the veil, a life of joy and peace. The earth shall soon dissolve like snow; the sun forbear to shine. But God, who called me here below, will be forever mine." (John Newton, "Amazing Grace", 1779).

Transports Québec

Welcome

When our travels on the
Highways and Byways of life
take us into uncharted territory,
under the best of circumstances, the
communities we discover will have
a welcome mat out, and the
mayor will be waiting to
give us the key
to the city.

We will pleasantly realize that we "are no more strangers and foreigners, but", instead, are "fellowcitizens with the saints, and of the household of God." (Ephesians 2:19).

In fact, the relationships we forge as we travel upon the Highways and Byways of Life prepare us for our eventual homecoming with our Heavenly Father. Even now, we can visualize it in our minds' eye. "Here you are, home from your mission. It seems like it was such a short time. Think of the people you met, the people you helped. Think of how you have grown spiritually. It seems like you were a child, so immature, when you left home such a short time ago. There is mother waiting to embrace you, standing just a bit behind father, who is bursting with pride. Are those tears of happiness on mother's cheeks? Father first strikes hands with you, then embraces you warmly. The feelings are resonant, and you know this is where you belong – this is a real homecoming – home to Heavenly Father and Mother." (Anonymous).

Welcome To A New Beginning

We
can't
start over
and make a
new beginning,
but we can begin
now and make
a new ending.

The Lord is in possession of the Master Plan, but He is still very willing to show us how to become the architects of our own fate. On the Highways and Byways of Life, He will lead us to a point where we draw a line in the sand, and declare, as did Joshua of old: "Choose you this day whom ye will serve, whether the gods which your fathers served that were on the other side of the flood, or the gods of the Amorites, in whose land ye dwell. But as for me and my house, we will serve the Lord." (Joshua 24:15). It is at that point, when we have committed ourselves to follow the covenant path, that He will reveal to us His divine design.

He will Welcome us To a New Beginning. To those who have forsaken the word, and in order for them to be spiritually aerobically fit, He will prescribe a spiritual heart transplant. Nothing short of that can maintain the lifestyle of the Saints.

Those who have had its physical equivalent find it necessary to take a cocktail of immunosuppressant medication, according to a strict regimen, for the rest of their lives. The same prescriptions must be taken, in specific doses, at the same time every day. The routine must be followed without variation, in order to avoid the risk of failure of the surgical procedure. All doctor's appointments must be kept, every recommended laboratory test must be performed, medication side effects must be monitored, and drug interactions and the signs and symptoms of organ rejection must be controlled.

The same anti-rejection protocols must be followed after we have spiritually been given new hearts and have been born again. If we are not vigilant in doing so, our new hearts will surely fail us. As the prophet Ezekiel declared: "A new heart also will I give you, and a new spirit will I put within you." (Ezekiel 36:26). To keep our new hearts from becoming cold and stony, we need to take a cocktail of immunosuppressant medication in the form of prayer, service, and temple attendance. We need to follow a strict regimen in the form of regular spiritually aerobic church activity. We need to be diligent with medication whose form and substance is found in Gospel ordinances.

if we want to jump-start our New Beginning, we must be diligent to maintain a schedule of regular accountability interviews with our spiritual physicians, and, in particular, to participate in the house calls that take the form of ministering visits to the poor in spirit. We must be alert to our need for regularly recurring repentance and learn to self-monitor the spiritual promptings that assure us we have received forgiveness of our sins and are thereby maintaining the health and vitality of our new hearts.

If we sense that our organ transplant has begun to fail, or if we feel that it is being rejected because of the effects of carnality, sensuality, or devilishness, we must know to whom we can turn for triage, for guidance and direction, so that the destructive elements might be decisively eliminated, in order to restore spiritual heart-health. We exercise diligence, because we want to be able to sing the song of redeeming love without experiencing shortness of breath.

No matter where we may find ourselves on the Highways and Byways of Life, we must strengthen our heart transplants by putting our shoulders to the wheel and pushing along. Cycling through the Standard works may seem repetitive, but it is one of God's favored spin classes. Studying the Come Follow Me program may seem daunting, but it establishes a habit pattern that can propel us over the summit of even the most challenging passes, those seeming obstacles to our progression.

Critics might see only frivolous repetition in our efforts to maintain spiritually aerobic health, mistaking repetition and reiteration for detachment from a worldly lifestyle that focuses on instant gratification. But God has a surprise in store for those who endure to the end in righteousness. Sooner or later, there will be for those of us who have had a spiritual heart transplant a moment in the sun, when the light of understanding illuminates our mind and confirms the divine potential of the new organ beating steadily in our chest.

As the morning breaks over the eastern sky, and the sunrise heralds another day, once again the self-evident truth will be gloriously confirmed: We have been born again. As we feel our new heart beating steadily in our chest, we will realize that we have given ourselves to the Savior. We will tangibly feel the spiritual element that sustains our forward momentum as we push along on the Highways and Byways of Life into the unexplored reaches of eternity. Our new hearts will not only have exposed us to an improved lifestyle, but they will also have sustained our lives. With all diligence, we will keep them vital and healthy, knowing that it is from our hearts that the fundamental issues of life flow, as in a revelatory stream. (See Proverbs 4:23).

WE RESERVE THE RIGHT TO REFUSE SERVICE TO ANYONE

We Reserve The Right To Refuse Service To Anyone

Our Heavenly Father has invited all of His children "to come unto him and partake of his goodness; and he denieth none that come unto him, black and white, bond and free, male and female; and he remembereth the heathen; and all are alike unto God, both Jew and Gentile." (2 Nephi 26:33).

"It's a beautiful day in the neighborhoods" we visit along the Highways and Byways of Life, and "a beautiful day for a neighbor." We feel to ask: "Would you be mine? Could you be mine? I have always wanted to have a neighbor just like you. I've always wanted to live in a neighborhood with you. So, let's make the most of this beautiful day. Since we're together, we might as well say, would you be mine? Could you be mine? Won't you be my neighbor? Won't you please, please won't you be my neighbor?" (Lyrics by Fred Rogers).

When the noise of the world gets in the way, and we post signs in our windows that tell passersby that We Reserve The Right To Refuse Service To Anyone, what has really happened is that we have forgotten who our neighbors really are. If we don't experience an attitude adjustment, it will be time to get out the body bags, because the inevitable casualties of war will soon begin to stack up. Our preoccupation with ourselves will deplete our energy, and we will find ourselves dealing with distractions we cannot control. Because of our shortsightedness, we will damage ourselves in ways both subtle and unexpected.

We cannot persist in intolerant behavior that relies on the corrosive elements of acrimony, anger, animosity, bitterness, fanaticism, hostility, rancor, prejudice, racism, sullenness, and vindictiveness toward others, without suffering self-inflicted wounds. All this can be avoided by following the simple admonition to love our neighbors as ourselves, which is one of the fundamental operational principles of The Plan of Salvation.

Mosiah knew who his neighbors were, and how he should treat them. The Savior was his mentor and the model for his behavior. He was ready to succor those that stood in need, and to provide for them of his own substantial means. He withheld judgment and assisted the poor, asking: "Are we not all beggars? Do we not all depend upon the same Being, even God, for all the substance which we have, for both food and raiment, and for gold, and for silver, and for all the riches which we have of every kind?"

(Mosiah 4:16-19). With neighborly love, he cast a benevolently blind eye on their supposed faults or shortcomings. His example taught that good intentions and empathy are not enough, and that our love for others needs to be as wide as the encircling arms of the Lord Jesus Christ.

Wheelchair Access

"There are no
ordinary people",
wrote C.S. Lewis. "You
have never talked to a
mere mortal." Instead, it
is immortals with whom we
interact on the Highways
and Byways of Life.
Thus, "our charity
must be a real
and costly
love."

Set in the grass alongside the road on the Highways and Byways of Life are mailboxes perched on posts. After the crash of the stock market in 1929 sent the world's economy into a free fall, itinerants who had been befriended by their more fortunate fellow-travelers marked their mailboxes with an "X." This simple scratch endured the wind, rain, sleet, and snow of a dozen winters during the Great Depression, and it spoke volumes. It was a hobo sign, universally recognized across the vast expanse of the country, alerting other riders of the rails that a hot meal and a piece of pie would always be waiting for them at the far end of a front walkway. The "X" acknowledged that someone recognized them, cared about them, and was prepared to help them in a tangible way. Even though they might be temporally

Meanwhile, "little people, like you and me, if our prayers are sometimes granted beyond all hope and probability, had better not draw hasty conclusions to our own advantage. If we were stronger, we might be less tenderly treated. If we were braver, we might be sent, with far less help, to defend far more desperate posts in the great battle." (C.S. Lewis, "The World's Last Night", p. 10-11).

Where am I?

No
darkness
is so dense
or menacing
or so difficult,
that it cannot be
overcome by light.

The Restoration has set in motion a number of protocols that have been designed to dramatically increase the amount of available light in the world, so its inhabitants can more clearly see the answers to life's greatest questions: Where did we come from? Why are we here? Where are we going? These measures generously provide more than enough illumination to go around. Heavenly Father has seen to it that every earnest seeker of truth will be able to read the fine print of the Gospel Plan and determine where they fit in. Its footnotes will snap into sharp focus. Its topical guide will intuitively begin to make more sense. The relevance of the whisperings of the Spirit, of the teachings of the Lord's prophets, and of God's written word, will become increasingly apparent.

Foundation principles will be coherently knit together by being stitched into an understandable pattern, and the witness of truth will be displayed upon a tapestry for all to see, without the need for external warrant.

This spiritual illumination is called "the Gift of the Holy Ghost." Its power surpasses the output that is simultaneously provided by the Light of Christ. Those who matriculate in the Lord's curriculum, and who enjoy guidance from both the Light of Christ and the Holy Ghost, experience a manyfold increase in their spiritual visual acuity. Whereas they may have been limping along in the shadows, discerning only dimly the path of progress along the Highways and Byways of Life, the tandem influence of guidance from heaven fills their bodies with illumination. They feel the comfort of increased protection from evil influences, and they experience a flush of excitement as they vanquish every foe with the simple weapons of light and truth. They savor the indescribable feeling of light penetrating to their nethermost parts. Their souls resonate with understanding, as when Joseph Smith received "The Vision" known as Section 76 of the Doctrine & Covenants. The prophet is said to have declared: "My whole body was full of light, and I could see even out at the ends of my fingers and toes." (Philo Dibble, "Journal").

Where Is Everybody?

As we travel the Highways and Byways of Life, and we gaze up at the stars, we look for signs of life, but we see none. We hear a great silence. This is the contradiction between the astronomically high estimates of the probability of extraterrestrial life out in the vast reaches of the cosmos, and its corresponding lack of evidence.

Early in 2012, NASA's planet-hunting Kepler spacecraft confirmed the discovery of the first alien world that lies within the habitable zone of its host star, where temperatures would allow liquid water to exist. From its launch on March 7, 2009, to the end of its mission on October 30, 2018, when it depleted its nuclear fuel, Kepler observed 530,506 stars and discovered 2,662 exoplanets.

The exciting thing about the discovery of that particular planet in 2012, though, is that it is a potentially habitable alien world orbiting a star very much like our own sun.

"In November 2013, astronomers estimated, based on Kepler space mission data, that there could be as many as 40 billion rocky, Earth-size exoplanets orbiting in the habitable zones of Sun-like stars and red dwarfs within the Milky

Way." "Wikipedia"). That number, again, is 40,000,000,000 potential "earths".

Using the High Accuracy Radial Velocity Planet Searcher (HARPS) spectrograph at the European Southern Observatory in Chile, astronomers have found within the Milky Way nine more similar planets only slightly larger than earth. The investigators estimate that about 100 such planets lie in the immediate neighborhood of the sun. The "new observations with HARPS suggest that about 40 percent of all red dwarf stars have an 'earth-like' planet orbiting in the habitable zone." (Space: On MSNBC.com on 3/28/2012)

It seems plausible that over billions of years, intelligent life should have flourished on at least some of these "M Class" ("Earth Similarity") planets that likely permeate our galaxy. The technological accomplishments of humans over the past 50 years, or 5 years, or even the last 5 minutes, beg the question: "Where Is Everybody?"

Wildlife Crossing

> We should try to be at least as
> obedient as J. Golden Kimball,
> who is reported to have said:
> "I may not always walk the
> straight and narrow, but
> I sure as hell try to
> cross it as often
> as I can."

Closely related to "Watch for Wildlife, is the sign that warns us of the "Wildlife Crossings" that we will surely encounter as we journey along the Highways and Byways of Life. "God doth not walk in crooked paths, neither doth he turn to the right hand nor to the left, neither doth he vary from that which he hath said, therefore his paths are straight, and his course is one eternal round." (D&C 3:2). But, we can be sure that many who are walking in darkness at noonday will cross our paths. They have no idea where they are going, and we would do well not to follow them.

In the pre-earth existence, when we were spiritual toddlers and were just learning how to walk the strait and narrow path, we must have taken our Father at His word when He assured us that "resistance" training would one day pay big dividends. When He urged us to do 10 push-ups through The Book of Mormon, we probably voluntarily tacked on another 13, all the way through the Articles of Faith.

Instead of bench-pressing only the Aaronic Priesthood, we added on the additional weight of The Oath and Covenant of The Melchizedek Priesthood, because we knew we'd need additional muscle fiber and strength down the road. When He asked us to get our heart rates up to a steady 75 verses a day to facilitate our comprehension of Gospel principles, we instead pushed our limits to whole chapters and even books of scripture. The elliptical trainer of consecration, the stationary bike of service, and the treadmill of sacrifice put us through the whole range of motion to develop and strengthen our core, and our reward was the increased capacity of our hearts to pump the life-giving element of the Spirit through our bodies. We knew that one day our hearts would enlarge to encompass empathy for our fellow men, and that our bowels would be filled with compassion as we witnessed their struggles.

We would have developed the power to live in the world, without being overcome by the wildlife constantly crossing our path, no matter how many times we wound encounter it, on the Highways and Byways of Life.

 国土交通省

Wind Gusts

> In the Last Days, as the Spirit
> withdraws in the face of increasing
> wickedness, hurricane force winds
> of destruction will rake the
> earth, and the righteous
> will find sanctuaries
> only by standing
> in holy places.

The faithful will enjoy "the power of God unto salvation" and become the architects of their own fate, in a very real sense. (Romans 1:16). They will be given the skills and the materials to build a temple in which to live their lives, rather than a shanty, in which they might only endure the vicissitudes of life. Which one it will be will depend on them. The outcome will be determined largely by their perspective. If they can face the Wind Gusts in their lives "with understanding, faith, and courage, they will be strengthened and comforted, and spared the torment which accompanies the mistaken idea that all suffering comes as chastisement for transgression." (Marion G. Romney, C.R., 10/64).

Sometimes bad things happen to good people, and life can be unpredictable. None of us can control the wind; it is one of many uncertainties with which each of us must deal. But if our foundation is solid and our footing is secure, we will be able to successfully adapt to circumstances and maintain our focus. When the rains descend, and the floods come, and the winds blow and beat upon our houses, they will not fall, for they will have been founded upon a rock. (See Matthew 7:5). We will "work out (our) own salvation with fear and trembling." (Philippians 2:12).

Winding Road

Why is it
that we can
sometimes simply
raise our eyes to heaven
and clearly see the visions
of eternity, but we cannot
look five minutes into
our future here
on earth?

Perhaps it is by divine design that our path is a Winding Road. We cannot see very far ahead or tell what the future will bring. Nor can we tell much about our past, for our birth is a sleep and a forgetting, and the soul that rises with us, our life's star, hath had elsewhere its setting, and cometh from afar." (Wordsworth).

"I wish I could remember the days before my birth," mused the poet, "and if I knew our Father before I came to earth. In quiet moments when I'm all alone, I close my eyes and try to see my Heavenly home. Although I can't remember and cannot clearly see, I listen to the Spirit and so I must believe. But still I wonder, and I hope to find the answer to the question that is on my mind. Where is Heaven? Is it very far? I would like to know if it's beyond the brightest star." (Janice Kapp Perry).

Work In Progress

There will be daunting
obstacles that threaten to frustrate
our progress along the highways and
byways of life. So, we had better make
sure that all of the resources we
will need are fully operational
before embarking upon the
next leg of our
journey.

Demosthenes overcame a lisp to become one of the greatest orators of all time. Beethoven composed some of his finest music after he had become deaf. Early in his career, Abraham Lincoln said: "I will prepare myself, and some day my chance will come."

"We need limitations to open our inner selves, dispel our ignorance, tear off disguises, throw down old idols, and destroy false standards. Only by such rude awakenings can we be led to dwell in a place where we are less cramped and less hindered by the ever-insistent external. Only then, do we discover a new capacity and appreciation of goodness and beauty and truth." (Helen Keller).

As a young man, Heber J. Grant couldn't carry a note. Later, he became well known for his singing abilities. He was fond of relating the observation of Ralph Waldo Emerson, to his own experience: "That which we persist in doing becomes easier for us to do; not that the nature of the thing is changed, but that our power to do is increased."

 **LIETUVOS AUTOMOBILIŲ KELIŲ DIREKCIJA**

WRONG WAY

Wrong Way

The Church
is a hospital
for sinners, to
nurse them back
into a state of
innocence.

When we have gone the Wrong Way on the Highways and Byways of Life, and we fall short of obedience to any of God's laws, the Atonement stipulates that we travel the Road to Repentance. This Requires that we act with Responsibility, as we Recognize the Reality of our transgression and view it with Revulsion, and experience Remorse that drives us to our knees. In our heart-felt prayers, we Relate to our Heavenly Father how we feel, in a process of confession that is the most painful example of Revelation. This demands that we Renounce our self-defeating behaviors, make Restitution to injured parties where possible, and then do whatever is necessary, as the Spirit directs us, to submit ourselves to a Refiner's fire that will help us to Re-establish a Reconciliation with heaven and Regain the Rapport with Jesus Christ that had formerly been our hope and our joy. As we Renew our Resolve to walk the covenant path, it will be through the miracle of the grace of Him Who is our Redeemer, that we will Receive a Remission of our sin.

Following the repentance process, recollections of our blackest deeds may surface in our memory, but only to serve the purpose of motivating us to hold steady as we strive to be better in the future. But the pain associated with our former sins will have been swallowed up in the Atonement.

The road to repentance is a path that all must follow as we negotiate the Highways and Byways of Life. It requires great courage, much strength, many tears, unceasing prayers, and untiring efforts. "There is no royal road to repentance, no privileged path to forgiveness." We must all follow the same course whether we are rich or poor, educated or untrained, razor sharp or of a slow wit, tall or short, prince or pauper, or king or commoner. "There is only one way.," but it is the right way. It is long road, spiked with thorns and briars and pitfalls and problems." (Spencer W. Kimball, "The Miracle of Forgiveness", p. 149). It may require that we travel a path leading to our own personal Gethsemane, on to Calvary, and then to a quietly empty Garden Tomb. It is a path that leads to our intended destination, and that makes our journey worth the effort.

Republic of Estonia
Road Administration

WRONG WAY GO BACK

Wrong Way Go Back

If we find ourselves doctrinally
dehydrated, intellectually inhibited, or
if we are experiencing a famine of faith
as we trudge along on the Highways and
Byways of Life, we should take courage
in the fact that light will always
trump darkness when they go
head-to-head against
each other.

In the scriptures, light is mentioned 453 times, while light and its contrasting element of darkness are linked together 103 times. One particularly vivid description of darkness is found in The Book of Mormon in the 8th chapter of 3 Nephi. These verses tell us that at the time of the crucifixion of Christ, "there was darkness upon the face of the land." (V. 19, see Matthew 27:51). In Book of Mormon lands, so overpowering was the murky blackness, so complete and total and universal was its influence, that "those who had not fallen could feel the vapor of darkness." (V. 20, see Exodus 10:21-23).

Not only the Holy Ghost, but also the Spirit of Christ seems to have been withdrawn. Thus, "there could not be any light at all." (V. 21, see D&C 84:45-46, & 88:7-13). The survivors of the spiritual storm that had swept over the countryside could see neither "the sun, nor the moon, nor the stars, for so great were the mists of darkness which were upon the face of the land." (V. 22).

Hopefully, this Book of Mormon record is as close as any of us will ever come to understanding just how overwhelming will be the spiritual darkness that will prevail among those who are resurrected to a kingdom without glory, which is as a "lake which burneth with fire and brimstone, which is the second death." (D&C 63:17). For the Sons of Perdition, existence in such a spiritual vacuum will be a living hell, where the prince of darkness will reign unchecked.

If we have been going the Wrong Way, through the power of the Atonement, we can always go back; although we may have walked in darkness, we can be guided by a great light; although, on the Highways and Byways of Life, we have dwelt in the land of the shadow of death, upon us the light may yet shine. (See Isaiah 9:2).

 Latvijas Valsts ceļi

Yield

> We use
> our agency
> best, when we
> surrender our
> will to that
> of God.

The Highways and Byways of Life were carefully constructed to create the conditions whereby, in an atmosphere of opposition within the crucible of mortal experience, we might use our agency to come unto Christ.

His Atonement makes it possible for us to make any of a wide range of choices regarding the path that we will follow, that will have consequences that vary from good to bad. The key is to allow Him to soften our telestial tendencies, that we might Yield our hearts to His better judgment, and to His unerring sense of direction.

We must pay no attention the crooner who sang: "And now, the end is near, and so I face the final curtain. My friend, I'll say it clear; I'll state my case, of which I'm certain. I've lived a life that's full. I've traveled each and every highway; and more, much more than this, I did it my way." ("My Way", lyrics by Paul Anka). What a pathetic waste it would be, if we arrogantly, haughtily, and proudly boasted that we had summarily declined the helping hand of God! Why would one want to celebrate their life's journey by declaring that they had done it alone! How could one be so egotistical as to think that their way was better than God's way?

If we do not Yield ourselves to His better judgment, we run the risk of becoming mired in a quicksand of monotonously repetitive underwhelming convention and mind-numbing conformity. If we surrender our will to God, however, He will bless us with imaginative spontaneity and refreshingly distinctive artistic individuality.

If we allow the hobnailed boots of indiscretion's marathon dancer to tap a rowdy two-step across the terracotta of our consciousness, if we allow excess to become our master, if we permit reason to be cast into the rumble seat of our libidinous juggernaut, we must equally accept the fact that the piper must eventually be paid! (See Pogo: The Cartoon Philosopher).

If we homogenize our mortal experience as we negotiate the Highways and Byways of Life by insisting that we do it our way, if we attempt to smooth out all the rough edges that have been wisely and providentially placed there by our Heavenly Father, we may inadvertently be neutralizing the very things that would have contributed most significantly to our happiness. If we do not Yield to powers that are greater than ourselves, we might run to and fro, and by so doing think that we are covering a lot of ground. But we will never come to know it would have been better to engage His way, and not our way, during our journey on the Highways and Byways of Life.

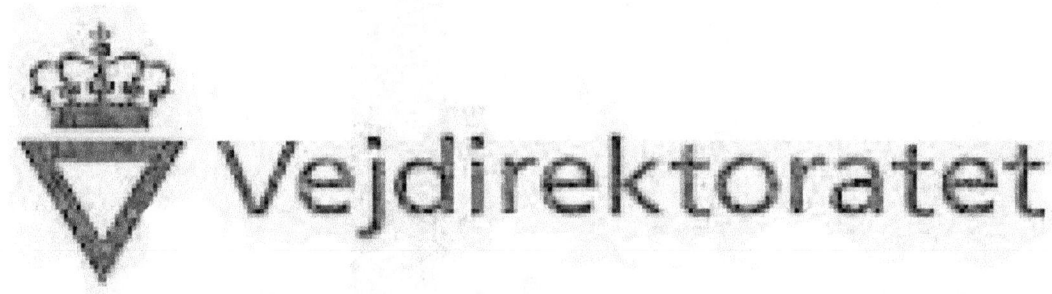

Yield To Oncoming Traffic

"Iniquity
had come upon the
people because they did
yield themselves unto
the power of Satan."
(3 Nephi 7:5).

We must never Yield To Oncoming Traffic on the Highways and Byways of Life, no matter the cost. Though all hell should endeavor to shake the promises we have made to our Heavenly Father, we will never, no never, we will never, no never, we will never, no never, no never forsake! (See "How Firm a Foundation", Robert Keen).

In Hebrew, to repeat something three times makes it superlative, as in "good," "better," and "best." In the case of the lyrics to the hymn "How Firm a Foundation", the word "never" is used, not three times, but seven times in succession. We must (1) never, ever, (2) under no conceivable circumstances, (3) on no occasion whatsoever, (4) at any time, (5) by no means, (6) in no way, (7) and on no account, allow the thought to crystalize in our minds to forsake our noble birthright.

Yield To Pedestrians Ahead

*Mortality was designed
with good reason to
be a journey that
was to be taken
by foot.*

For most of recorded history, walking has been the primary means of transportation all over the world. If we spend too much time traveling at 75 mph in the fast lane of the Highways and Byways of Life, we will miss the essence of what could have been a profoundly enjoyable experience. The Savior walked all over Galilee, but there is only one reference in the scriptures that he ever traveled by any means other than foot. (See John 12:14 & Matthew 21:7). The Apostle John declared: "He that saith he abideth in (the Savior) ought himself also so to walk, even as he walked." (1 John 2:6).

Walking is good for our bodies. In addition to journeying by foot, work, cleanliness, rest, and exercise are important and positive components of the Word of Wisdom. Therefore, the Lord commanded: "Cease to be idle; cease to be unclean; cease to find fault one with another; cease to sleep longer than is needful; retire to thy bed early, that ye may not be weary; arise early, that your bodies and your minds may be invigorated." (D&C 88:124). In the end, "they that wait upon the Lord shall renew their strength; they shall mount up with wings as eagles; they shall run, and not be weary; and they shall walk, and not faint." (Isaiah 40:31).

Afterword

As we negotiate the
Highways and Byways of Life, the
one element that stands out as an
unparalleled aid to travelers is
The Book of Mormon.

On one occasion, Helen Keller offered this wise counsel: "I who am blind can give one hint to those who see: Use your eyes as if tomorrow you would be stricken blind. And the same method can be applied to the other senses. Hear the music of voices, the song of a bird, the mighty strains of an orchestra, as if you would be stricken deaf tomorrow. Touch each object as if tomorrow your tactile sense would fail. Smell the perfume of flowers, taste with relish each morsel, as if tomorrow you could never smell and taste again. Make the most of every sense; glory in the beauty which the world in all the facets of pleasure reveals to you through the several means of contact which Nature provides. But of all the senses, I am sure that sight is the most delightful."

Rather than multiplying mirrors, The Book of Mormon increases the light by which the children of God may see, not only with their eyes, but also with their spiritual sixth sense, to navigate past the doctrinal dead-ends and the conceptual cul-de-sacs on the Highways and Byways of Life.

We are confined to a world of our own making, but most of us are trapped within the narrowly defined perceptual prisons we have created for ourselves. Its walls are reinforced with the razor-wire of limiting beliefs, those stories we tell ourselves that cause us to sabotage our own best efforts. They can damage and even cripple our lives, diminish our abilities, compromise our progress, and prevent us from attaining our goals. Although all of us have limiting beliefs, everyone has the power to change them. Most people, however, don't realize it's possible, and for that matter, aren't even aware that they have made conscious decisions about what they choose to believe and not to believe.

This book, and in fact, our testimonies themselves, rely upon The Book of Mormon to provide the rebar that can help to build bridges of understanding that can make our passage along the Highways and Byways of Life not only pleasant, but also inspirational.

I hope that you, dear reader, can appreciate how the Restoration of the Gospel is an indispensable aid to navigation as we negotiate traffic delays, detours, and other unanticipated obstacles on the Highways and Byways of Life. The resources of the Restoration include, but are not limited to the following: A fifth Gospel (3 Nephi) summarizing Christ's ministry in the New World, the fulfilment of the prophecies of Ezekiel and Isaiah, the elements of singularity that distinguish Latter-day Saints from all other Christian denominations, the well-defined lines of demarcation that separate those who make their home in Idumea from those who embrace the Gospel, as well as the symmetry, balance, harmony, clarity, focus, and purpose that flow out of an increase in spiritual illumination.

The resources of the Restoration include the stories of inspiration that touch us individually, as well as collectively. These resources include truth in its untarnished majesty, the invention and innovation of the Light of Christ, the unrestrained influence of the Holy Ghost, and a powerful witness that Jesus Christ is not only our protector but also the generator of life itself,

The resources of the Restoration include a standard by which the Bible may be interpreted, doctrine that is a weapon more powerful than military might, and clear definitions of the Savior's might, majesty, power, dominion, and authority.

In a violent world, they include uninhibited access to the horns of sanctuary, and the continuing mercies of God, Who blesses us with the means to find our way home, there to obtain His Rest.

The resources of the Restoration provide us with a reiteration of the definition of baptism; they equip the army of God with superior firepower as it teaches the nations, give us confidence to strategically preach the Gospel from a unique perspective, allow us to draw upon the life experiences of mentors who have had similar challenges, present us with a blueprint for survival in difficult times, and bless us with understanding, to familiarize ourselves with the mysteries of the kingdom which are the saving principles and ordinances of the Gospel.

The resources of the Restoration bless us with a profound spiritual insight to know who we are, and they teach us to be stewards who recognize and accept the responsibilities of accountability.

The resources of the Restoration bless us to feel the sweet miracle of forgiveness through a comprehensive understanding of the Atonement of Jesus Christ. His sacrifice, and our repentance, free us from an unrelenting bondage to sin, so that we might no longer be held hostage by guilt.

The resources of the Restoration bless us with knowledge, which is powerful. Declared Helen Keller: "Rather, knowledge is happiness, because to have broad, deep knowledge is to know true ends from false, and lofty things from low. To know the thoughts and deeds that have marked our progress is to feel the great heart-throbs of humanity through the centuries; and if we do not feel in these pulsations a heavenward striving, we must indeed be deaf to the harmonies of life." ("The Story of My Life").

This abundance gives us the courage to take risks; to break free from the security nets and comfort zones in which the timid apprehensively squeak out their lives, scurrying from one shadowy refuge to another. We finally understand that emulating the Savior means following the Savior to the

Celestial Kingdom by way of Gethsemane. Willingly, then, we surrender our agency to Christ, knowing that it is a necessary and vital step on our path of progress along the Highways and Byways of Life that leads to heaven.

Appendix One

It is really quite
amazing how often the road
signs that line the Highways and
Byways of Life are mentioned
in the scriptures. Listed in
this Appendix are just a
few of them, for you
to thoughtfully
consider.

"I
will
harden
Pharaoh's heart,
and multiply my
signs and my wonders
in the land of Egypt."
(Exodus 7:3).

"This is the
sign which the
Lord hath spoken."
(1 Kings 13:3).

"Hezekiah
said unto Isaiah, What
shall be the sign that the
Lord will heal me?"
(2 Kings 20:8).

"In those days
Hezekiah was sick
to the death. And he
prayed unto the Lord;
and he spake unto him,
and he gave him a sign."
(2 Chronicles 32:24).

"Thine enemies roar in the midst of thy congregations; they set up their ensigns for signs."
(Psalms 74:4).

"They shewed his signs among them, and wonders in the land of Ham."
(Psalms 105:27).

"The Lord himself shall
give you a sign."
(Isaiah 7:14).

"I and the
children whom
the Lord has given
me are for signs and
wonders in Israel."
(Isaiah 8:18).

"I will set a
sign among them."
(Isaiah 66:19).

"Learn not the
way of the heathen,
and be not dismayed
at the signs of heaven;
for the heathen are
dismayed at them."
(Jeremiah 10:2).

"I have set thee for a sign unto the house of Israel." (Ezekiel 12:6).

"I gave them my sabbath, to be a sign between me and them." (Ezekiel 20:12).

"I thought
it good to
shew the signs
and wonders that
the high God hath
wrought toward me."
(Daniel 4:2).

"In those
days there shall also
arise false Christs, and false
prophets, and shall show great
signs and wonders, insomuch,
that, if possible, they shall
deceive the very elect.
(J.S.T Matthew 1:22).

"Then certain
of the scribes and of
the Pharisees answered,
saying, Master, we would
see a sign from thee."
(Matthew 12:38).

"The Pharisees also
with the Sadducees came,
and tempting, desired him
that he would shew them
a sign from heaven."
(Matthew 16:1).

"Ye can
discern the
face of the sky, but
can ye not discern the
signs of the times?"
(Matthew 16:3).

"A wicked and
adulterous generation
seeketh after a sign."
(Matthew 16:4).

"And as he sat
upon the mount of Olives,
the disciples came unto him
privately, saying, Tell us, when
shall these things be? And
what shall be the sign of
thy coming, and of the
end of the world?"
(Matthew 24:3).

"He that
betrayed him
gave them a sign,
saying, Whomsoever
I shall kiss, that same
is he. Hold him fast."
(Matthew 26:48).

"When shall these things be? And what shall be the sign when all these things shall be fulfilled?" (Mark 13:4).

"And these signs shall follow them that believe." (Mark 16:17).

"And this shall be a sign unto you; Ye shall find the babe wrapped in swaddling clothes, lying in a manger."
(Luke 2:12).

"And others, tempting him, sought of him a sign from heaven."
(Luke 11:16).

"This is an
evil generation.
They seek a sign,
and there shall be
no sign given it."
(Luke 11:29).

"And they asked
him, saying, Master, but
when shall these things be?
And what sign will there
be when these things
shall come to pass?"
(Luke 21:7).

"Then
answered the Jews
and said unto him,
what sign shewest thou
unto us, seeing that thou
doest these things?"
(John 2:18).

"Then said Jesus
unto him, Except ye see
signs and wonders, ye
will not believe."
(John 4:48).

"They said therefore unto him, What sign shewest thou then, that we may see, and believe thee?"
(John 6:30).

"And many other signs truly did Jesus in the presence of his disciples, which are not written in this book."
(John 20:30).

"And I
will shew wonders
in heaven above, and
signs in the earth beneath;
blood, and fire, and
vapour of smoke."
(Acts 2:19).

"By the hands of the
apostles were many signs
and wonders wrought
among the people."
(Acts 5:12).

"He brought them out, after that he had shewed wonders and signs in the land of Egypt, and in the Red sea, and in the wilderness forty years."
(Acts 7:36).

"The Lord ... gave testimony unto the world of his grace, and granted signs and wonders."
(Acts 14:3).

"Through
mighty signs and wonders,
by the power of the Spirit of God;
so that from Jerusalem, and round
about unto Illyricum, I have fully
preached the gospel of Christ."
(Romans 15:19).

"For the Jews
require a sign, and the
Greeks seek after wisdom."
(1 Corinthians 1:22).

"Truly the signs
of an apostle were
wrought among you in
all patience, in signs, and
wonders, and mighty deeds."
(2 Corinthians 12:2).

"And I saw
another sign in heaven,
great and marvellous."
(Revelation 15:1).

"This thing shall be given unto thee for a sign." (1 Nephi 11:7).

"The Lord himself shall give you a sign." (2 Nephi 17:4).

"And after the Messiah shall come, there shall be signs given unto my people of his birth, and also of his death and resurrection."
(2 Nephi 23:6).

"Show me a sign by this power of the Holy Ghost, in the which ye know so much."
(Jacob 7:13).

"And many signs, and wonders, and types, and shadows showed he unto them, concerning his coming." (Mosiah 3:15).

"Korihor said unto Alma: If thou wilt show me a sign, that I may be convinced that there is a God, yea, show unto me that he hath power, and then will I be convinced of the truth of thy words." (Alma 30:43).

"This
will I give
unto thee for a
sign, that thou shalt
be struck dumb."
(Alma 30:49).

"There are many
who do say: If thou
wilt show unto us a sign
from heaven, then we shall
know of a surety; then
we shall believe."
(Alma 32:17).

"And it came to pass that they did have their signs, yea, their secret signs, and their secret words; and this that they might distinguish a brother who had entered into the covenant."
(Helaman 6:22).

"I give unto you a sign; for five years more cometh, and behold, then cometh the Son of God."
(Helaman 14:2).

"I will give
unto you for a sign
at the time of his coming;
for behold, there shall be
great lights in heaven."
(Helaman 14:3).

"There began
to be greater signs and
greater miracles wrought
among the people."
(3 Nephi 1:4).

"There began
to be lyings sent forth
among the people, by Satan, to
harden their hearts, to the intent
that they might not believe in
those signs and wonders
which they had seen."
(3 Nephi 1:22).

"The
people began to forget
those signs and wonders
which they had heard, and
began to be less and less
astonished at a sign or
wonder from heaven."
(3 Nephi 2:1).

"Nine years had passed away from the time when the sign was given, which was spoken of by the prophets, that Christ should come into the world."
(3 Nephi 2:7).

"They did show forth signs also and did do some miracles among the people."
(3 Nephi 7:22).

"The
people began
to look with great
earnestness for the sign
which had been given by the
prophet Samuel, the Lamanite."
(3 Nephi 8:3).

"I give
unto you a sign,
that ye may know
the time when these
things shall be about
to take place."
(3 Nephi 21:1).

"And these signs shall follow them that believe."
(Mormon 9:24).

"There shall be greater signs in heaven above and in the earth beneath."
(D&C 29:14).

"I am
God, and
mine arm is not
shortened; and I will
show miracles, signs, and
wonders, unto all those who
believe on my name."
(D&C 35:8).

"Faith cometh
not by signs, but
signs follow those
that believe."
(D&C 63:9).

"He that
believeth shall
be blest with signs."
(D&C 68:10).

"Unto you
it shall be given to
know the signs of the
times, and the signs
of the coming of
the Son of Man."
(D&C 68:11).

"And
the Gods
organized the
lights in the expanse
of the heaven, and caused
them to divide the day from
the night; and organized
them to be for signs."
(Abraham 4:14).

Appendix Two

Within Appendix
Two are lists of the road
signs that appear alongside the
Highways and Byways of Life. These
are found in Volumes One, Two,
and Three of this series. When
you find more, as you surely
will, think about how they,
too, can provide insight
into our experiences
as we journey on.

Volume One

Accident Ahead
Adopt a Highway
Amateur Radio Zone
Amish Using Roadway
Apply Parking Brake Before Leaving Vehicle
Are We There Yet?
A Shoulder to Cry On
Battery Charging Station
Battlefield
Begin Higher Fines Zone
Be Prepared to Stop
Better Times Ahead
Beware of Monsters
Beware of Trolls
Beware of Warnings
Beware of: Well, Just Beware
Bike Lane
Blasting Area: Turn Off Two-Way Radios
Blind Driveway
Blind Person Area
Blowing Dust Area
Breakup Limits
Bridge Closed
Bridge May Be Icy
Bright Futures Ahead
Buckle Up
Caution: Approaching Train
Caution: Be Alert for Cyber-Terrorists
Caution: Bear in Area
Caution: Men Working Above
Caution: Speed Bumps Ahead
Caution: Student Driver
Caution: Water on Roadway During Rain
Cemetery Entrance
Chain Up Area
Changed Priorities
Changes Ahead
Children at Play
Click It or Ticket
Commercial Vehicles Prohibited
Complications Ahead
Confused?
Construction Zone
Crossing Guard on Duty
Cross Traffic Ahead
Cross Traffic Does Not Stop
Currency Exchange
Damaged Goods
Danger: Do Not Touch
Dangerous Crosswinds
Danger: Stay Behind Guard Rail
Danger: Strong Currents
Danger: Three Guesses What It Is

Danger: Watch for Falling Debris
Dead End Road: No Turn Around
Deaf Child at Play
Delayed Rewards Ahead on Right
Deposit All Rubbish in Receptacles Provided
Destination Ahead
Detour
Difficult or Dangerous Terrain Ahead
Diversion
Diversity
Divided Highway
Divided Highway Ends
Do Not Enter
Do Not Feed The Unicorns
Do Not Pet the Fluffy Cow
Do Not Pick Up Hitchhikers
Don't Be Stupid
Don't Drink and Drive
Drop Off Point
End School Zone
End Detour
End Roadwork
Eyes on The Road
Falling Rock
Family Restroom
Frequent Stops and Backing

Fire Station
First Aid Cabinet
Flexibility
Flooded
Forgiveness Ahead
Fork in Road
Form Single Lane
Freeway Ends
Fresh Oil
Frost Heaves
Fun Zone Ahead
Game Crossing
Garbage Collection
Gas, Food, & Lodging
Give 'em A Brake
Go Faster
Going South on Route 666
Golf Cart Crossing
Good, Better, Best
Good Things Take Time
Go / Stay

Volume Two

Handicap Parking
Highway to Hell
Highway Widening
Historical Marker
H.O.V. Lane Ahead
How's My Driving?
I'm Sorry
Irreconcilable Differences
It's Just the Beginning
Joyride Through Idumea Next Left
Keep Going
Keep Moving Forward
Keep Right
Keep Right Except To Pass
Lane Deviation
Lane Ends Merge Right
Left Lane Closed
Left Lane Ends Merge Right
Left Lane Exits
Lighted Pathway Ahead
Lights On For Safety
Limited Sight Distance
Loading Zone
Local Deliveries Only
Local Traffic Only
Long And Winding Road Ahead
Long Winter Blues Ahead

Low Flying Aircraft
Low Overhead Clearance
Ludicrous Speed
Maintain Top Safe Speed
Maternity
May Be Icy Ahead
Men At Work
Merge Right
Merging Traffic
Metered Parking
Move Over for Emergency Vehicles
My Way or The Highway
Neonatal Unit
New Life / Old Life
New Road Layout Ahead
New Signal Ahead
Next Mood Swing: 6 Minutes
No Cell Phone Zone
No Drones
No Engine Brakes
No Heavy Loads
No Honking
No Idling Allowed
No Left Turn
No Littering
No Motorized Vehicles
No Parking Except During Church Services
No Parking on Pavement

No Parking Stopping
 Standing Anytime
No Parking Taxi Stand
No Parking Tow Away Zone
No Passing Zone
No Services
No Shoulder
No Stopping Or Standing
No Thru Traffic
Notice: Tutorial on Faith
 Ahead
No Tolls
No Trash
No Turn On Red
No U Turn
No Waiting Anytime
Obey Flagman
Oncoming Traffic Does
 Not Stop
One Way: Do Not Enter
One Way System
Only You Can Prevent Wildfires
Open Range
Pain Relief Just Ahead
Parallel Parking
Pass With Care
Pastor Parking Only
Past, Present, Future
Pavement Ends
Picnic Area

Pilot Car: Follow Me
Please Look Both Ways
 Before Crossing
Please Turn On Your
 Headlights
Practice / Theory
Primitive Road Not
 Maintained
Private Road Local Access
 Only
Public Access Area
Push to Enter
Questions / Answers
Quiet: Hospital Zone
Reality Check Ahead
Recreation Area
Recyclable Waste Only
Reduced Speed Ahead
Reduced Visibility
Rest Area Ahead
Resume Speed
Rewards Just Ahead

Volume Three

Right Turn Only
Road Closed
Road Closed to Thru Traffic
Road Ends
Road May Be Icy
Road Narrows
Road Narrows
Rough Road Ahead
Roundabout Ahead
Rumble Strips Ahead
Scenic Byway
School Bus Stop Ahead
School Zone
Secure Your Load
See Tracks / Think Train
Severe Weather Shelter
Share The Road
Sharp Curves
Sidewalk Closed
Signal Ahead
Signal Operation Changed
Slight Curve Ahead
Slippery When Wet
Slow
Slow: Blind Curve Ahead
Slow: Construction Ahead
Slow Down
Slow Down at Night
Slow Down: Obey Speed Limit
Slow Down: Uncontrolled Intersection Ahead
Slow Down: Only You Can Prevent Speed Bumps
Slower Traffic Keep Right
Slow: Road Under Repair
Slow: Rough Road Ahead
Slow Vehicles Use Right Lane
Smiles to Go Before We Sleep
Speed Cameras
Speed Checked by Radar
Speed Limit
Speed Reduced Ahead
Speed Up
Stay Awake
Stay in Your Lane
Steep Grade Ahead
Stop Ahead
Stop Complaining
Stop Distracted Driving
Stop Drowsy Driving
Stop Gossiping
Stop Grumbling
Stop, Look, and Listen
Take Responsibility
Thank You Foer Slowing Down
The Future: Just Ahead
Think Before You Speak
Thru Traffic: Merge Right
Tough Decisions Ahead
Tow Away Zone

Traction Tires Required
Traffic Fines Double in Work Zones
Traffic Islands Ahead
Train Depot
Try Your Brakes
Trucks & Heavy Vehicles: Balance Your Load
Trucks: Right Lane Only
Turn On Headlights For Safety
Two Way Traffic
Under Construction
Uneven Road Surface
Unplanned Detour
Use Headlights in Tunnel
Viewpoint Ahead
Vision Just Ahead
Visitor Information
Warning: Avalanche Area
Warning: I Do Dumb Things
Warning: I May Look Calm
Warp Drive
Watch Downhill Speed
Watch For Congestion Ahead
Watch for Emergency Vehicles
Watch For Farm Machinery
Watch For Oncoming Traffic
Watch For Pedestrians
Watch For School Bus
Watch For Wildlife

Wedding Season Ahead
Weigh Station
Weight Restriction Notice
Welcome
Welcome to a New Beginning
We Reserve The Right To Refuse Service To Anyone
Wheelchair Access
Where am I?
Where Is Everybody?
Wildlife Crossing
Wind Gusts
Winding Road
Work In Progress
Wrong Way
Wrong Way – Go Back
Yield To Oncoming Traffic
Yield To Pedestrians Ahead

About The Author

Phil Hudson and his wife Jan have 7 children and over 25 grandchildren. They enjoy spending time with their family at their cabin nestled in the Selkirk Mountains, on the shore of Priest Lake, the crown jewel of North Idaho. Phil had a successful dental practice in Spokane, Washington for 43 years, before retiring in 2015. He has an eclectic mix of hobbies, and enjoys the out of doors. He always finds time, however, to record his thoughts on his laptop, and understands Isaac Asimov's response when he was asked: If you knew that you had only 10 minutes left to live, what would you do?" He answered: "I'd type faster."

Phil received the inspiration to write this book while he and Jan were serving as missionaries for The Church of Jesus Christ of Latter-day Saints, in the Kingdom of Tonga. While there, they celebrated their 50th wedding anniversary.

By The Author

Essays

- Volume One: Spray From The Ocean Of Thought
- Volume Two: Ripples On A Pond
- Volume Three: Serendipitous Meanderings
- Volume Four: Presents Of Mind
- Volume Five: Mental Floss
- Volume Six: Fitness Training For The Mind And Spirit

First Principles and Ordinances Series

- Faith - Our Hearts Are Changed
- Repentance - A Broken Heart and a Contrite Spirit
- Baptism - One Hundred And One Reasons Why We Are Baptized
- The Holy Ghost - That We Might Have His Spirit To Be With Us
- The Sacrament - This Do In Remembrance Of Me

Book of Mormon Commentary

- Volume One: Born In The Wilderness
- Volume Two: Voices From The Dust
- Volume Three: Journey To Cumorah

Doctrine & Covenants Commentary

    Volume One - Sections 1 - 34
    Volume Two - Sections 35 - 57

Minute Musings: Spontaneous Combustions of Thought

    Volume One
    Volume Two
    Volume Three

Calendars:

    As I Think About The Savior
    In His Own Words: Discovering William Tyndale
    Scriptural Symbols

Children & Youth

    Book of Mormon Hiking Song
    Happy Birthday
    Muddy, Muddy
    The Hiawatha Trail: An Allegory
    The Little Princess
    The Parable of The Pencil
    The Thirteen Articles of Faith

Doctrinal Themes

    Are Christians Mormon? Volume One
    Are Christians Mormon? Volume Two
    Christmas is The Season When...Volume One
    Christmas is The Season When...Volume Two
    Dentistry in The Scriptures
    Gratitude
    Hebrew Poetry
    Hiding in Plain Sight
    One Hundred Questions Answered by The Book of Mormon
    The Highways and Byways of Life Volume One
    The Highways and Byways of Life Volume Two
    The Highways and Byways of Life Volume Three
    The House of The Lord
    The Parable of The Pencil
    Without The Book of Mormon
    Writing on Metal Plates

A Thought For Each Day of The Year

    Faith
    Repentance
    Baptism
    The Holy Ghost
    The Sacrament
    The Sabbath
    The Plan of Salvation
    Life's Greatest Questions
    Revelation
    The Atonement
    The House of the Lord

Professional Publications

    Diode Laser Soft Tissue Surgery Volume One
    Diode Laser Soft Tissue Surgery Volume Two
    Diode Laser Soft Tissue Surgery Volume Three

These, and other titles, are available from online retailers.

Quid magis possum dicere?

www.ingramcontent.com/pod-product-compliance
Lightning Source LLC
Chambersburg PA
CBHW060508240426
43661CB00007B/957